HUMILITY

and
How I *Almost*
Achieved It

Uncovering a Highly Undervalued Key
to Lasting Success and Kingdom Power

Ben R. Peters

Humility and How I *Almost* Achieved It
© 2013 by Ben R. Peters

Published by
Kingdom Sending Center
P. O. Box 25
Genoa, IL 60135

www.kingdomsendingcenter.org
ben.peters@kingdomsendingcenter.org

ISBN 13: 978-0-9789884-8-7

Cover image:
Cover and book design by *www.ChristianBookDesign.com*

Contents

Chapter One

Why This Subject is Normally Off-Limits to Talk About

There's an old joke that goes like this: I just wrote a book called, "Humility, and How I Attained It!"

My title is, of course, a take-off on that joke.

But why is it funny? It's funny because everyone knows that if you actually achieved humility, you wouldn't write a book boasting about it. You would just be proving that you really had not achieved it.

A DIFFICULT SUBJECT TO WRITE ABOUT

The whole idea of writing about humility is intimidating and somewhat of a risk. First of all, anyone checking it out would think, "Who would be crazy enough to think he is an expert on humility?" It's definitely a lot easier and safer to joke about it than to deal with it as a serious subject to share with your peers.

It's like someone saying, "I know I'm extremely beautiful or good looking!" Even if you were, people would look down on you for your pride and arrogance. Basically, to be successful in life and have good relationships, we make a point of trying to avoid appearing to be proud or arrogant. Instead, we try to impress people in more subtle ways. Claiming humility is actually a very non-subtle way of proving we are proud.

So it's obviously not a smart idea to pretend to be an expert on this subject, because God is not the only one who hates pride. Most people despise anyone who thinks they know it all or have it all together—especially if they think they are holier than everyone else. My only claim to being anything close to an expert is that I have been taught by experience the nastiness of my pride and God has had to continually deal with that ugly part of me.

And it's not because I have anything to be proud of! I discovered long ago that pride is a disease that infects the total population of the globe and that even the poorest folk in developing nations find things to be proud of, wanting you to compliment them on their most meager possessions. It is really amazing to witness.

Secondly, the devil understands the power of humility and how it can be employed against his kingdom. He hates people discovering that power for themselves. He will try to use anything in his toolbox of tricks to perpetuate our life of pride, and he will certainly attack anyone promoting this agenda of humility. After all, we know that it was pride that brought him down and sentenced him to eternal damnation. He wants us to be like him and achieve the same end result if he can. That's why he makes it so hard to both apologize and forgive. Both require humility and he would rather promote the bitterness and anger that come out of pride—the pride that he introduced into Heaven and then the earth.

Thirdly, if we take on the challenge of extolling the virtues and blessings of humility, God may allow us a few extra opportunities to see the ugliness of our pride to help us illustrate the need for humility as we write the book. There's nothing like personal examples to illustrate the point you want to make. It's the last thing I feel like doing, because I really don't want to humble myself that much and expose my flesh to others. I'd much rather tell you about all the miracles God has done through my ministry. But, of course, that just shows how much I need to learn to practice what I'm going to be preaching in this book.

Now, if I could just use my wife as an example and talk about how much she needs to be humbled! But then, probably no one would believe me, and besides, I'd have to answer to her. Then we'd both have to humble ourselves again. Actually, I have to say that we have been learning the blessings of humbling ourselves to the point where it's not as hard as it used to be. I don't know if it will ever really get easy, but there's always hope as long as we're still breathing.

Finally, all kidding aside, this book is really not about how humble I am or how much pride I've had to deal with; rather, *it's about the ways of the Kingdom. If we want to show our love to our Savior and Lord, and build His Kingdom, we need to learn from His teachings, and His example, how to position ourselves for promotion for His glory and honor.*

We will never be able to reveal the greatness of our God, nor will be ever be able to accomplish anything significant for the Kingdom of Heaven on this earth if we don't highly value and pursue this elusive entity we call humility. God wants to promote us more than we want to be promoted, but without true humility, we will do ourselves and His Kingdom more harm than good. He wants to promote us so He can more powerfully use us. Without humility, we may appear to be successful, but we won't make Him famous without His grace, which only comes to the humble. And our own fleeting success will prove to be an empty thing, filled with plenty of sorrow and pain.

SO WHY TAKE THE CHANCE OF GETTING KILLED TO WRITE THIS BOOK?

No, I really don't get excited about martyrdom or suffering for Jesus. I don't want to be judged, criticized or ostracized. I like being accepted, admired and honored. What is it then? Am I just lacking good judgment or basic intelligence? I hope not, although some who know me might vote for that option.

I write about humility for the same reason I write about any other subject. God has entrusted me with revelation and information from His heart. I have been asked to steward some of the revelatory gems that He is releasing on the earth for the end time harvest. I have a mandate, a responsibility and a privilege.

That may sound like a statement of pride, but when you understand what humility and pride really are, you understand it really isn't a statement of pride, because I know I didn't earn or deserve this assignment. I got it because of His grace and because He wants to get the message out to others. True humility is not saying you are lower than dirt and uglier than a mud hen. It is acknowledging the goodness of God and knowing with a grateful heart that He created you and designed you for a purpose. Because of His goodness and love, you and I can accomplish things for His glory and help others to know and love Him like we do.

The subject of true humility is incredibly important and will become increasingly so as God's Kingdom expands on the earth in these exciting days of harvest. There is no character quality that is more crucial for the successful administration of His Kingdom throughout the earth. You may have never thought of humility as having such a prominent role in God's plans and purposes, but I believe it is my very serious mandate to tell you why that is the case and how you can better pursue this great and powerful resource in your glorious adventure with God.

It is my sincere belief that very few Christians, including leaders, have any idea of how many ways pride manifests and how many problems it creates in God's Kingdom, especially in what we call, "the church." At the same time, we have little idea of how much we could accomplish if we could kill our pride and embrace humility.

I also believe that because of pride's many disguises, we have little understanding of what true humility looks like. Often, as I mentioned above, we mistake self deprecation as humility, when it's really just another form of pride. A poverty mentality can also be seen as a form of humility, but with me it was a manifestation of my own ugly pride. It doesn't matter how pride manifests—God has to resist it. That's not a good thing for us and our attempt to build His Kingdom. I'd rather enjoy His grace than His resistance and I know I will be much more successful in my pursuits when He is extending His hand of grace, rather than holding up His hand to resist me.

WHO IS MORE HUMBLE?

I was born and raised in Canada. Our family was not wealthy by any means. Our Mennonite heritage blessed us with a simple and frugal lifestyle and a dislike of those with a high and haughty attitude. I resented the rich and arrogant and that resentment manifested itself every so often, but I didn't realize that I had a problem with pride myself. If you said I was sophisticated, that would have been an extreme insult to me. Looking at America and Americans as a Canadian, I was convinced that they were a proud nation that felt superior to everyone else and I judged them in my heart for that.

As I matured and experienced a powerful personal move of God, I began to see the wickedness of my own heart. God in his sense of humor brought a wonderful American girl, named Brenda, into my life. Two years after finishing my formal education, we moved into the United States. There I observed some of the cultural differences between Canada and the USA, as well as the differences between my own family's culture, as opposed to Brenda's family's culture.

I finally made a thoughtful analysis of the difference between the USA and Canada. I concluded that Americans were proud, and they were proud of it. On the other hand, Canadians were humble, and they were proud of that.

There are few things as subtle as pride and our pride actually and naturally gets in the way of our ability to see it. Pride throws up many road-blocks to our ability to see how devious it really is. You can try to kill it as often as you want, but the ugly thing keeps reviving and catching you by surprise.

PURPOSE FOR WRITING

I shared above that the reason for writing was my calling and responsibility, etc. I want to add to that now and more specifically declare what I believe is the purpose in God's mind for having me take the risks involved to write this book.

Every true Christian wants to please God and accomplish what they are called to do on this earth. But our walk with God gets extremely difficult at times and we get so discouraged with ourselves and our failures. We try to do what we know is right, but like Paul in Romans 7, we often do what we don't want to do and fail to do what our heart really wants to do. We carry shame, guilt and condemnation, while trying not to let others know how much we struggle. We don't want to be rejected by other Christians, who seem to be doing a whole lot better than us. Unknown to us, however, they are having just as many problems as we are.

But God has a solution and it really works. It's pretty simple, but not very easy. It not only helps us be successful in our spiritual walk, but it unleashes great power to accomplish awesome exploits for God. It's the key to open the door of God's grace. Without His grace, we have nothing of value and can do nothing worthwhile.

GOD'S RULES

Since God has written the rules and enforces them, we must play by His rules if we want to win. His rules include His promise that He gives grace to the humble and resists the proud.

The divine purpose and plan of God for this book is to inform and remind His children that they can be winners and champions if they read His playbook and play by His rules. It's harvest time and God is looking for people He can trust to operate His powerful harvesting equipment, which is His power and authority manifesting through His spiritual gifts. He can't safely and freely give these tools to those who don't know how to use them properly.

This is the reason for this book from God's perspective. Those who embrace humility as a wonderful treasure will be positioned as high as their humility will allow them to go. Those who cannot humble themselves will find themselves on the sidelines, wishing they could get in the game.

GOD'S PRIORITIES ARE NOT OURS

I had an interesting experience while serving as a part-time associate pastor in Oregon. I worked a few months, just before Christmas, for a young married man from our church, who was managing an electronics store while still only about twenty-one years old. I was a few years older and he confided in me that he was having a serious problem with pornography. I liked this young man a lot, but he had other issues that were revealed as I worked for him. The biggest issue was a kind of cockiness and self-centeredness. I was being taught by the Holy Spirit in those days about how much God hates pride, so I tried to share a simple truth with him.

I suggested that, contrary to our normal thinking, and as destructive as pornography can be, God was more concerned with his pride than his pornography. If he could further humble himself and deal with his pride, God would give him grace to overcome his moral issues.

My friend didn't want to hear about it. He was sure that pride was not his problem. He just wanted me to help him get rid of the issue that made him feel guilty. I told him that most Christians who struggle with any typical negative habit, such as smoking or drinking, often wanted to get delivered for the wrong motive.

They wanted freedom from the bad habit, mainly so that they could feel better about themselves and shake the guilt and condemnation they felt. They also wanted to be just as spiritual or righteous as the other church people who seemed to have it all together and were in good standing with the leadership and qualified for official positions in the church. I felt that God often did not deliver them instantly because they would just become like the Pharisees, full of self-righteous pride. But if He left them in the battle with their habit, it would keep them from getting too proud, and perhaps He could use them in a greater way than if they were delivered and self-righteous.

I did pray for my friend, but I was wishing he would heed my advice. I knew God was actually more concerned with his pride than his problem with pornography. I know that is not the way we normally think, but believe me, God's thoughts are not the same as ours. I've been blessed with a number of encounters with God where He was dealing with my pride, and God blessed me with a family that raised me in the Word from the womb. After over sixty years of knowing God and His Word, I have no doubt that my pride is more offensive to Him than any of my other weaknesses.

I can confirm that by the way He deals with me. Yes, He lets me know if I slip up in some other area, but it always comes back to the fact that I have to humble myself to get out of a bad situation. He works through any kind of circumstances in amazing ways, just to let me know that my pride is a hindrance to our relationship and to my personal success in this world. In His mercy and love, He keeps a short leash on me.

Chapter Two

Humble Beginnings in Learning to Be Humble

DEFINING HUMILITY

I seriously considered making the effort at this point to formally define humility before going into a deeper discussion of the subject. However, I have concluded that such a definition will evolve as we tell our story and share insights on the subject.

RELATIONSHIP BETWEEN POVERTY AND HUMILITY

When someone mentions their humble beginnings, they are usually talking about their lack of resources such as finances and family reputation. They may begin their story telling of just how poor they actually were. They may have lived through a time of drought and famine, such as happened in the 1930's.

They will say that they had a very humble existence and survived on rations and the sharing of their possessions with each other.

This use of the term "humble" does not actually or necessarily mean that they were humble. Even though they lived simply and in poverty, it doesn't mean that they had a humble heart.

However, those who grew up in that impoverished lifestyle did not have the same battle with pride as those who grew up in affluence and wealth. It's true that they could easily develop a pride in their poverty, but they would seldom act in such an obnoxious or arrogant way as people who grew up thinking that they were better than others because of the power of their wealth.

The Bible frequently warns about pride in association with wealth. Jesus even made the statement, "Woe to the rich!" (Luke 6:24). He said that they already had their reward. What was their reward? They had material things, of course. But they also had the power that their money provided and the honor people had to show them because of their position.

James writes, "But you have dishonored the poor man. Do not the rich oppress you and drag you into the courts? Do they not blaspheme that noble name by which you are called?" (James 2:6, 7)

Obviously, Jesus and James are generalizing, but the facts are clear. Rich people have a battle with pride and arrogance that poor people don't have. Thus they have a different battle to fight than the poor, but the poor also have their own battle with pride, which can be just as big a hindrance to Kingdom success as the pride of the rich. However, to be clear and truthful, the Bible seldom points out the pride of the poor, like it does of the rich.

MY OWN HUMBLE BEGINNINGS

My own "humble" beginnings story is somewhat similar to most of the population, but definitely unique in a lot of ways. We had never starved and never went without clothes to wear, but I had to wait for Friday (my dad's payday) for a nickel to buy an eraser. We had the basics, but I know we were certainly not what we would call middle class today, unless there is a lower than lower middle class.

My wonderful parents were actually missionaries, although they never left North America. They had landed in Canada as immigrants from Mennonite communities in Russia, shortly after the Communist Revolution. They did apply to be missionaries to Africa, but after all the Bible School training, followed by six months of missionary nursing training, they were rejected because my mother's heart was apparently not up to the harsh challenge of going to Africa in the early 1940's.

They decided to be missionaries anyway and journeyed northward by train in British Colombia to a little town where they had heard some people from Germany had settled to begin farming in the Peace River Valley. German was their native language and the people who had come from Germany were apparently not born-again Christians. They arrived with at least one child, not knowing a soul in the region and without any outside support.

My father found work taking care of someone's farm or ranch. Eventually he built a small cabin where my brother, Dave, and I were born. Dave became a full-time missionary in Latin America, serving in three different countries. I have a missionary's heart, but have lived mostly in the USA and Canada.

I have, however, taken over twenty-five ministry trips to foreign lands and actually was the only one of my siblings to make it to Africa, where I have enjoyed the privilege of at least partially fulfilling my parents dreams.

As you can imagine, we were anything but rich in earthly goods. We came from a line of very industrious, hard-working German Mennonite families, but as missionaries, our parents lived by faith and served God with all their hearts, making every sacrifice necessary to further God's Kingdom. We certainly didn't have the battles that wealthy families have when it comes to pride. But, yes, we certainly had pride, especially religious and intellectual pride.

PRIDE IN BEING RIGHT

Our family's Mennonite heritage included a belief in pacifism—that is the teaching that Christians should not go to war and kill people. Long before I was born, our family's theology had changed to full-blown Pentecostalism, but my parents still clung to the pacifist doctrine. They were taught never to kill for any reason. I, personally, do not subscribe to that doctrine myself when it comes to defending my country or my family.

Even though we had a theology of not killing others, we would certainly enjoy long back and forth arguments. We did develop sharp and sarcastic tongues, but it became more of a game than a serious conflict. We liked to see if we could come up with better or sharper sarcasm than our friends and relatives. I still observe this going on in good fun among some of my friends and family.

The most relevant point here is that I, for one, hated to be wrong. When I felt I was right, I would argue endlessly and never surrender what I knew I had seen or done. It was a stubborn form of pride and to this day, my flesh loves to be right. Saying, "I was wrong," is getting easier, but it has taken awhile.

Being raised in a family with a history of academic achievers, we all took pride in our intelligence. I have since learned that there are many different types of intelligence, not just the type that intelligence tests test. However, whether we had money or stylish clothes meant little to me compared to whether I was smart or right. I cared little about money or style, but you didn't call me stupid. I took great pride in my academic accomplishments.

RELIGIOUS PRIDE

Religious pride is probably the most obnoxious to God and to the world outside the church. You don't have to be rich or even intelligent to wallow in this one. As I shared in the story of my experience with my young friend who had the battle with pornography, we can become "spiritual" for all the wrong motives and then get proud of it, causing others to run away from God instead of towards Him.

Our Mennonite heritage left lots of room for this form of pride to grow and reproduce in its successive generations. It's the same thing I see in so many denominations today. We see our group or movement as having more truth or accomplishments than others, thinking we are right where others are wrong. We interpret the Bible correctly, while the doctrines of others are full of errors.

In the Mennonite tradition, the German language was

hallowed and traditional customs were revered. Many varieties of Mennonites arose as a result of divisions in theology and favored practices. Some became much more legalistic and clung to the old ways more rigorously than the branch that my parents grew up in, which was the Mennonite Brethren. However, as they pursued the teachings on the Fullness of the Holy Spirit and Healing in the Atonement, they were no longer allowed to stay in the Mennonite church and began a journey of finding their place elsewhere in the Kingdom of God.

Other Mennonite groups became known as the Amish, Pennsylvania Dutch, Hutterites, etc. Most of their followers resisted all modern conveniences and tried to keep the old ways of previous generations. Perhaps you have seen horse and buggies driven by men and women dressed in black, especially in certain rural areas in Indiana, Pennsylvania and other states, as well as some of the provinces of Canada, including Alberta, where I attended high school.

Although they live the simplest and "most humble" lifestyle, they certainly have a major battle with the kind of pride that Jesus confronted in the Pharisees. You experience a similar situation in Israel with the most orthodox Jews, whose attire lets you know they are from a very "spiritual" group.

MY "SPIRITUAL" CHILDHOOD

Like every child, I wanted affirmation and attention. I liked almost all sports, but was never great at anything. I liked school and was always in the top 5% or so of my class. But for me, I found out the easiest way to get affirmation was to be the most spiritual.

To be honest, I did have a desire to know God and His Word, and I have to give the credit to Him and to my parents who gave all of us the opportunity to excel in "spiritual" things. But along with the God-given desire to know Him and serve Him, my own personal motivation for gratification got mixed in with the good and pure.

I could read well at a young age and I could memorize fairly quickly and methodically. Since we usually had kids clubs at church and Daily Vacation Bible Schools in the summer, I would easily win most of the contests by memorizing or reading the most Scriptures, or reciting the sixty-six books of the Bible in order.

We also had frequent sword drills, where the leader would first say, "Swords Present" (where the accent is on the "sent" and the "s" is pronounced like a "z"). We would hold up our closed Bibles and he would say the "address" of a Bible verse, such as, "I Chronicles 7:14". We would have to keep holding our Bibles high in the air until he gave the command, "FIGHT!" The first one to find the Scripture would begin to read it out loud. It was fun, especially when I could win much of the time.

On top of the admiration and the awards I would win at competitions, I also had another motivation for being "spiritual." My mother decided to reward us and motivate us to memorize Scripture. As mentioned earlier, there was little extra money after feeding a family of six on a linotype operator's salary, but she started us out at one penny per verse. (We had moved to North Battleford, Saskatchewan, when I was four and my dad got a job working for the weekly newspaper when I was six). I don't remember my siblings taking this offer very seriously, but I sure did. The good thing was that she agreed to raise our earnings to two cents the second year, three cents the third year and four cents the fourth year.

By the fifth year, I was into my teens, now living in Coaldale, Alberta, and memorizing larger portions of Scripture which I also used to gain rank in our Sky Pilots Christian Boys Club. Soon I was outranking the older teens and young adults who were actually the leaders of the club, patterned after military rankings. The ranks were gained mostly by memorizing Scripture, including some larger sections, such as John 3:1-21, Isaiah 53:1-2, and Philippians 2:5-11. Now I was not only gaining rank, but making pretty good money for a kid from a pretty poor family.

This had become a problem for my mother, who was stretching the budget already. She finally had to say, "No more raises!" I had to settle for the four cent per verse wage for the rest of my school days.

One year, when I was about twelve or thirteen years old, I decided on my own that I would memorize Matthew 2 for the church or Sunday School Christmas program. I memorized all twenty-three verses and recited them flawlessly before the whole church. I will always remember the feeling inside when I heard people tell my parents how amazing I was.

One warm Sunday morning after my senior year of high school, I got tired of listening to the preacher and decided to count how many verses I had memorized in my childhood. I counted almost a thousand. It took the whole sermon to add them up.

Although my parents never paid me to read the Scriptures, I did that on my own for bragging rights. I wanted to be able to say that I had read the whole Bible, which I did pretty much every year of my school days. I would religiously (pun intended) read every "begat" and "son of" in the Bible, and every law in the book of Leviticus. I was honest to a fault with facts, but I was also developing a strong "religious" pride in my accomplishments.

Of course, God had His hand on my life and I did enjoy His presence in worship and special revival meetings. When I heard a great preacher like Billy Graham, I wanted to be like him. I remember pretending to preach while using our outhouse. In a big family with a small house, that was a good place to be alone so no one would hear you. For the younger generation, an outhouse is what we used for a bathroom in the old days, before running water was available.

Nowadays, we have similar portable units hauled to construction sites and outdoor fairs, etc. to handle the needs when there are more people than available toilets. But when I was very young, that was our normal bathroom and you had to go outside to use it. We bathed in a large metal bucket or even a barrel when more convenient. Water was hauled and heated, but there was no tap with running hot water.

Getting back to the subject at hand, I had found my way to be recognized and affirmed by adults. I was doing things that were considered very "spiritual" by the grownups in my world. I was somewhat different from the other kids in many ways because of our different beliefs (we didn't square dance or have a family doctor, other than Jesus, and we didn't accept vaccinations). I didn't mind being different as long as I could be recognized and affirmed for something. My niche was a combination of excelling in academics and "spiritual" activities.

That's how I survived internally and that's how God prepared me to be a "teacher" of His Word. It was also a "Divine Setup" for God to teach me the ugliness of my own pride, including my "spiritual" pride.

THE PERFECT TRAP

I was an over-privileged child when it came to spiritual formation. I had been prayed over in the womb. My parents taught me to live by faith and they knew God and the Scriptures. They motivated me to read, learn and memorize. They taught me to stay away from sinful things. They warned me never to smoke the first cigarette or drink the first beer. They said the second and third one would never be a problem if I didn't take the first one. I heeded their wisdom and advice on those issues.

But the enemy, whose first sin was pride, had succeeded in putting me into a prison of my own pride. He had created the perfect trap and long before I was ready to go to Bible College and Seminary, he had caught me in it. Because much of my "spiritual" activities were motivated by my own need for security and affirmation, I had all the externals of spirituality, but my personal relationship with God was still quite shallow.

Since my intimacy with God was not my primary focus and passion, I did not have the inner strength to overcome the attack on my moral character that was to come against me in those wonderful transition years, commonly known as puberty. This attack was much more difficult to survive than any temptation to smoke or drink beer. It was an attack that caught me by surprise in the alone times in my life.

I never walked away from God or changed the "spiritual" practices in my life. I was just as interested in being honored for my spirituality as ever. But I was caught in a big battle. My mind and body were engaged in continual warfare. I hated to feel guilty and unclean, but I didn't have power to overcome the temptation, although I confessed and prayed frequently about it.

This was my dilemma and the enemy's trap:

1. My identity and acceptance socially was based on my "spirituality."
2. My struggle was in secret, so I could still appear "spiritual."
3. If I asked others for help I would lose my identity and acceptance.
4. My guilt and lack of self-worth grew.
5. My compromised heart needed healing and I was less able to help others.
6. I was in a trap created by my own spiritual pride and I couldn't get out.
7. If I had talked to someone, they would probably have told me how normal my problem was and given me keys as to how to deal with it, but I didn't have the courage to talk to anyone about it.

My struggles continued through my teen-age years and on into Bible School. But God in His mercy met me there at the campus of Canadian Bible College, which was in the process of becoming Canadian Theological Seminary.

It was in the late fall of 1965 that the Spirit of God invaded my life and turned it around into a life of joy and victory. As I look back on those days almost fifty years ago, I realize that the change in my life was a result of God's mercy and a decision I had to make. The decision was whether to protect my pride or to humble myself.

The decision had nothing to do with my moral weakness. It had everything to do with my pride—especially my spiritual pride.

I've told this story many times and in two or three of my books, but never before from this point of view.

THE MOST IMPACTING DECISION I HAVE EVER MADE

It was prophesied recently by Rick Joyner that we will be making small decisions in these days that will have huge implications for the future. That's exactly what happened in my life.

The setting was our small dorm room with two small beds, two small desks, a couple of bookshelves, and two small closets. The occasion was an officially scheduled dorm prayer meeting, which was held probably once a month for the purpose of helping us to share each others' burdens. Eight students filled the room to pray for various needs in the group. I was one of the lowly freshmen. One of the upperclassmen led the prayer meeting.

He asked the question: "Does anyone have any burdens?" This was spiritual lingo for, "We need some things to pray about because this is a prayer meeting and I'm supposed to get everyone praying."

It was just the normal thing to say, but it didn't hit me that way. It hit me instead like a ton of bricks or a sharp sword through my heart. The Holy Spirit took those words from my dorm-mate and spoke to me before I could answer. He spoke clearly to my heart, "You don't have any burdens!"

I knew right away it was true. I was truly enjoying my life at Bible School. For the first time since my pre-school days, I was surrounded with people who loved God and wanted to serve Him like I did. There were great teachers who challenged our hearts and minds, which I loved. There was great social life and good sports activities to get involved with. I had a new level of personal freedom which I had never had at home with parents and a grandmother telling me what I could or couldn't do.

Yes, the Bible School had rules and some balked at them, but for me, it was freedom, compared to my home life. I still struggled with moral issues, but I had been dealing with them for so many years that I had pretty much learned to push that part of my life into a back closet and keep the door closed as much as possible.

But, in all the good times I was enjoying, I knew the Holy Spirit was right. And as much as I like to be right and make explanations or excuses when I appear to be wrong, I knew better than to argue at that moment. After all, I was in a prayer meeting, and I was trying to feel spiritual, so I could pray a prayer that sounded as spiritual as the reputation I had tried to promote for myself. I did recognize the voice of the Holy Spirit and knew I could be in trouble if I ignored Him.

The statement, "You don't have any burdens" meant that I was self-centered, thinking about myself instead of others who had needs and problems. I knew God cared and had burdens for others. Many of the prophets in Scripture talked frequently about the "burden of the Lord" for some city or nation.

Since my whole family was Christian and in good health, and most of my real friends were as well, I spent little time praying for others. I knew that I should pray for the lost and for people who were sick. I should have more of a burden and spend more time in prayer for those who were not so well off as myself. So I made the decision to agree with God that I was missing His mark and needed to make some changes.

MY ANSWER

The leader of the prayer meeting starting asking each young man, going around the room in a clockwise direction. I was the fourth or fifth one to share my burdens. I had agreed with God, but now I was going to have to say something to the group that would reaffirm my reputation or destroy it. I could have come up with something for a prayer request, but I made an instant decision to be honest and respond to the voice of the Holy Spirit and humble myself before my peers, no matter what the cost.

I responded to the question by saying, "My burden is that I don't have one." I don't remember how anyone in the room responded. I don't remember anything else that happened that evening. I don't know what anyone thought of me after I humbled myself before the group. But I certainly do know what God did for me in the days, weeks, months and years that followed.

MY TRANSFORMED LIFE

Immediately, God began to answer my request for His burdens. The schedule at CBC was well laid out. Between 6:00 AM and 6:30 AM we were allowed in the halls and bathrooms for showers, etc. From 6:30 AM to 7:00 AM we were to be in our rooms for devotions. By 6:30 you were out of luck if you wanted to use the bathrooms. At 7:00 AM breakfast began and by 7:45 you were in your first class.

Thus, everyone was encouraged to spend time with the Lord and His Word for thirty minutes before breakfast. But God was doing something so powerful in me that I could not work with that schedule. For one thing, I was raised Pentecostal, praying out loud and often in tongues as well. My roommate was quiet and non-Pentecostal and I had no freedom to really pray like I desired in the room while he was there.

The biggest issue was the time restriction. I quickly realized that I needed the freedom to pray for a longer period of time and as loud as I needed to. God began waking me up around 5 AM and earlier. I would dress and slip out of the room to do my bathroom duties and then take my Bible next door to the main administration building where the chapel and classrooms were located. The cafeteria and piano practice rooms were in the basement and that's where I headed every morning for several months.

I was taking voice lessons and had my favorite little practice room, just big enough for an old piano and bench and two or three people standing up if they needed to practice a group number. That hallowed place was my Mount Horeb, my secret closet where I met God and He met with me. That was where my life was transformed and I found out how powerful my God really was.

God led me to the book of Acts day after day and week after week. I had thought that I should have a burden for a few people in my world. Instead, He gave me a burden for HIS people, HIS CHURCH!

I would come into the room and lay my Bible on the piano bench opened at the book of Acts. Usually, I read the first fourteen chapters one day and the second fourteen chapters the next day. I would get on my knees and read and weep. I began to see things from God's perspective.

God had given His church all the power they needed to expand His Kingdom and make Him famous in all the earth. Somewhere in the process of time, we had lost or given up that power and it made God very sad. I could feel the pain in His heart that His church was so content to do church meetings but never experience the power He gave to the early church that brought lost souls into His Kingdom .

I saw the Church of the Living God as a powerful giant in the earth, but it was fast asleep and ignored by the busy little people with all their selfish ambitions and with all their enormous problems in life. For much of society, the church had already become more of a nuisance than a blessing. We were a voice of judgment and condemnation, but had little supernatural power to fix any of their problems and help them change their lives for the better.

The world could see the religious pride of the church, but they couldn't see the love of God and the power of God to fix the huge problems they were facing. As I read about the power of the early church, I would weep and my tears would fall on my open Bible. I would pray for individuals, but mostly I prayed for the church in general and the churches I knew, where the meetings were uplifting and stimulating, but no one was crying out with passion for the kind of revival that would flip the power switch back to the "on" position in our churches.

Without fully understanding what I was doing, I was exercising the prayer of identificational repentance. I was repenting for my own lack of burden and also for that of our leaders and spiritual fathers in our churches from previous generations. Mostly, I was crying out for revival—for God to do it again, like He did back then.

During those months of deep intercession for the church, I experienced many personal blessings and learned many spiritual truths.

The first thing I learned was that the thesis of this book is true. The Bible works! When God says, He puts down and resists the proud and gives grace to and exalts the humble, He really means what He says.

HOW IT WORKED FOR ME

This was demonstrated to me in what happened in my life in those days.

First, my thought life had pulled me down so much for so long and I had prayed, resisted, and read the Bible for victory with no lasting results. I absolutely needed an infusion of God's grace. After humbling myself by admitting my weakness to my peers in response to the sweet convicting power of the Holy Spirit, the battle was over.

During those days of passion for revival and restoration of God's church, I experienced total relief from sexual temptation. It was definitely supernatural and a work of God's grace. Nothing else had brought the supernatural infusion of God's grace, and as far as I know, there is only one Biblical requirement for receiving God's grace—humility.

Another thought occurs to me. God says He resists the proud. I had a lot of religious pride in my life as a teen-ager. Perhaps God even resisted my prayers for victory over my moral failures because of my pride. If He had made it easy for me, it may have only increased my pride. That in turn would have made me more critical of others who were not as "spiritual" as I was. This dynamic also would have clearly applied to my young friend I mentioned earlier.

Second, I was normally a pretty positive person and generally quite happy, but after my breakthrough into some basic humility, my joy in life went to a much higher level than I had ever experienced before. Bearing God's burdens was at times intense, but never so heavy that it broke me down. His yoke is easy and His burden is light (or fits well) (Matthew 11:30).

It was always a very sweet time in which I felt His presence so near. I felt like I was weeping with Him, not on my own. I truly felt yoked together with Him. I never felt like I was making a sacrifice or being a martyr. It was nothing like when I was reading multiple books of the Bible in one setting for bragging rights. It was a time I truly looked forward to. It was the best time of the day.

MISSING BREAKFAST

There were numerous times when the burden of the Lord was on me that I was still in the little piano practice room when the breakfast bell rang at 7 AM. The presence of the Lord and His burden were still covering me and I resisted the inviting sound of the other students noisily gathering in the cafeteria just a few yards outside the door of my room. I had never fasted on purpose to that point, and I wasn't trying to fast. I just wanted to stay in that presence a little longer. There would be no food served again until lunch, but that mattered little.

Whenever the burden of the Lord would lift, a powerful wave of joy would flood my being. Suddenly, I became very light and full of the overflowing joy of the Lord. I would go through the day floating three feet off the ground (figure of speech). Nothing could take away this joy.

PASSING THE TEST

This miracle of God's grace was tested a number of times. My roommate, a senior, who was finishing a music degree, liked to keep the room very warm, while I preferred to keep it on the cooler side. With the old steam-filled radiator heaters it was difficult to control the temperature in the room. When it got too hot, the inside window could be lifted up. The outside storm window had three little holes about one and a half inches in diameter, that could be opened up to let in a little frigid Saskatchewan air to cool the room off. Incidentally, we often stored little bits of food that would have needed refrigeration between the two windows and they stayed chilled most of the school year.

One afternoon I came back to our room on a break and the room felt way too warm for comfort. My roommate was not there and I had no idea when he'd be back. I opened the window and let in some of the heat out and the cold air in. It was just getting comfortable when my roommate, who may have been having a bad day, returned to the room. He felt the crisp air blowing in when he opened the door.

Marching straight to the window, he covered the holes and slammed the inside window down and sat down at his desk without saying a word, but stress and anger were written all over his face. At that point, I experienced something totally foreign to my own nature. It was supernatural grace and compassion. I would naturally have been resentful and angry in return, but instead I felt so sorry for him and prayed silently for him.

I don't remember saying anything. I just remember the feeling I had for him and how abnormal it was for me. I knew it was not me or my nature. It was the supernatural nature and grace of God. Where did it come from? I can only assume it came in response to that same original act of humbling myself and other similar acts that followed it.

The third and most wonderful of all the unexpected benefits of humbling myself and sharing the burden of the Lord with Him was the wonderful and lovely young lady that came into my life at that time. Brenda had come from a much different background than mine. She had never been introduced to the ministry of the Holy Spirit or spiritual gifts. But her hunger and thirst for more of God had been stimulated in some of the classes.

Meanwhile, I had been studying and writing a paper about praying in the Holy Spirit. I had read numerous wonderful books on prayer and was overflowing with excitement about revival and the supernatural power of the Holy Spirit. I was full and she was hungry. God brought her to me to release something in her and then He began to let me know that she was going to be more than a friend.

It was in those days that God began to speak to me clearly about decisions I had to make by making some Scripture come alive when I read it. It would always be a clear "rhema" word from God. That's the kind of Word that faith comes from (Romans 10:17). That's how God directed me to propose to her on December 2, 1966, from the book of Isaiah.

On August 11, 1967, we were married in Seattle, Washington, and now have ministered together for more than forty-five years. I would never have guessed that making a quick decision to humble myself before my peers would end up resulting in God providing for me the wife of my dreams. If I had not been in a state of revival and overflowing with Heaven's joy and love, she would have never been attracted to me. I had nothing else to offer her but my faith and passion for God and His power.

RUTH—A BIBLICAL EXAMPLE OF HUMILITY'S REWARDS

I recently wrote a very small book called *The Boaz Blessing*. In this book I released a revelation regarding the blessing that came to Ruth from Boaz because of her sacrifice for Naomi, her mother-in-law. Ruth demonstrated incredible humility in leaving her own country and family because of her compassion for Naomi. She then humbled herself to go gleaning in the field of Boaz.

But Boaz heard about her sacrifice and showed great favor to her. She fell at his feet and cried out, "Why have you shown me such favor, since I am a foreigner?" Boaz expressed what I believe God would say to us. "It's been fully reported to me all that you have done . . . The Lord repay your work and a full reward be given you by the Lord God of Israel under whose wings you have come for refuge."

God has a record of every sacrifice and humble service on His behalf and He promises to repay and reward you for these sacrifices.

Ruth then humbly asked for more favor and Boaz kept adding favor and blessing until he actually married her and she became the great grandmother of King David. She went from being a poor widow in Moab, and then being a foreigner because of her humble sacrifice, to being in the lineage of David and Jesus and having a book written about her, which is published in the world's best-selling book, the Bible.

What a beautiful example Ruth is to us! But what an encouragement she is to anyone who has chosen to pursue humility!

The following chapter will reveal that, although I had made an important step toward humility, and although I had seen incredible rewards, I had not achieved a totally humble heart.

Chapter Three

Learning Humility from Failure

As weeks and months passed, God kept the fire alive in my soul. I returned to my little prayer closet on a regular basis and continued to cry out for revival and restoration in God's church. I loved prayer and believed in its power, especially after reading many classic books on prayer by people like D. L. Moody and R. A. Torrey. At some point I also read the book *Reese Howells, Intercessor*.

My passion for prayer led me to attend every available prayer meeting on campus. The Bible College, which had a strong missionary emphasis, divided the world into many regions and assigned one prayer band to each region. We would meet some time in the afternoon once a week. I remember that my first assignment was the Middle East. We prayed for the Jews and the Arabs in these countries, while Old Jerusalem was still in the hands of the Arabs.

After my revival experience, I was not satisfied praying for just one mission field and doing it just one day of the week. Different prayer bands met on different days and I would find where they were meeting and join one of them just about every day of the week. I would pray passionately for the missionaries and the people living in darkness all around the world.

PRIDE RESURFACES

While in these prayer meetings, I began to be annoyed by the lack of passion in the other members of the prayer band. If they prayed at all, their prayers seemed weak and shallow. It seemed they were praying just because it was their duty. They had no passion for the lost people going to hell. In my heart I became critical and judged them for being so unspiritual.

This attitude began to carry over into other aspects of Bible College life as well as church. It was very gradual and very subtle, but the mixture was polluting the purity of my walk with God and my brothers and sisters in Christ. I still had the anointing to pray passionately for revival in my prayer time, but outside the prayer room, I was more and more frequently finding fault with the apathetic church.

I had now become (in my own mind) the standard of what a Christian should be like. Instead of setting the standard with Bible reading and memorization, I was setting the standard with my prayer life. What I had begun in the Spirit through an act of humility, I was gradually transitioning into walking in the flesh in a religious spirit of pride. You see how sneaky and devious our enemy is and how he hates humility.

But God was merciful, understanding my immaturity and

continued to honor the level of humility that I was still pursuing. He began to give me some wonderful revelation from Scripture on the subject of faith and some of it became the basis for my Master's thesis a few years later.

FIRST TASTE OF REAL REVIVAL

Another incredible blessing and reward for one simple act of humility and the faithful follow-through was the joy of experiencing two different revivals or moves of God's Spirit. The first was there in Regina, Saskatchewan, where I was still in my seminary program. A revival team, led by the Sutera Twins, Ralph and Lou, came down from Saskatoon, where they had held explosive nightly meetings for eight weeks.

The first meeting in Regina was in our Seminary chapel, right above the little piano practice room where I had prayed daily for months, crying out for revival. The team then began to hold revival meetings in one of the larger church facilities in town, called Hillsdale Alliance. These meetings went on for six weeks before the growing revival team began to answer calls from all across Canada, the USA and Europe.

It was a revival of repentance, restored relationships and restitution of things stolen, including the cheating on income taxes. Cold and lukewarm Christians became on fire for God. Teens and parents were seen hugging and confessing to one another, tears streaming down their faces. Meetings were almost completely without preaching. Instead the evening was filled with emotional testimonies of God's work in the lives of people who had come previously and met God—usually in the prayer room. Upon hearing what God did for others, new people would say,

"If God could do that for them, He could do it for me, too." And off to the prayer room they would go to meet God. The meetings usually shut down around mid-night and were followed by "afterglows," which could last another two hours or so.

This was very gratifying to me, even though it had been several years since those passionate prayers for revival. By this time I was married, studying and working part time on the side. I was also serving as a weekend pastor in a little country church in Parry, Saskatchewan. My passion for revival had faded somewhat, but when the Sutera Twins came to town, it was quickly rekindled.

GREATER GLORY FALLS IN ARGENTINA

The second revival I was blessed to have a part in was in the fall of 1973. The man of God I had spent a year with in Albany, Oregon, in 1968/69, had been invited to Argentina for a series of meetings that would last six weeks. God led him to ask me to join him on this adventure. I personally believe that had I not had that personal revival, following one simple act of humility, I would never have found myself in Argentina in 1973.

Upon receiving the invitation, my wife, Brenda, who was already more prophetic than either of us realized, knew instantly that I was to go, even though it would mean more hardship for her. We already had one child and were functioning as foster parents to a five-year old boy. She went to stay with her parents for those six weeks. It was actually a very difficult time for her because of certain things going on in the family at the time, and we had never been separated for more than a day or so since getting married six years earlier.

But what an amazing time I had in the glory of all-out revival. The worship was so incredible and unlike anything I had ever experienced. It was full of passion and hunger for God. Songs were repeated many times to get the truths they were singing from the head to the heart, and in the smaller afternoon meetings in their Bible College, the choruses were interrupted frequently by passionate prayers, often with tears streaming down the faces of the person praying.

The evening meetings were incredible and I would have to say that they were the closest I have ever been to being in the early church in the first few chapters of the book of Acts. People were flocking to the front to receive Jesus, just as they flocked to the front to receive His healing touch, usually brought there by specific words of knowledge by our mentor, Elmer Burnette. I was so blessed to have him for a spiritual father in those days.

Elmer was a big man with a big heart. He was always open to praying for people and God had given him an amazing seer gift. When someone came for prayer, he would see pictures or videos of their life and tell them what Jesus wanted to say to them. There, in Argentina, I saw scores of pastors weep at the knowledge that God knew them and cared about their hardships and sacrifices, etc.

Elmer also had a wonderful gift of healing and a powerful deliverance ministry. He entered the ministry in his thirties with no Bible School. He learned to fast and pray and read his Bible, until God would give him something to say to the people. Then, without understanding spiritual gifts, he would receive words of knowledge about people, which always turned out to be accurate and fruitful when he would share them.

In the larger meetings, where people would crowd out the

public hall until many were standing outside the building, we would see dozens healed every night. Each night after the healings an altar call would be given for salvation and then for the baptism of the Holy Spirit. Elmer would always remind the people that he was not healing anyone. They must keep their eyes on Jesus, or the miracles would stop happening.

After three and one half weeks, the leaders decided to give us a break from two meetings a day and we drove up into some mountains for a little rest. However, we so enjoyed the amazing daily miracles that we were happy to get back to the meetings. By the time the six weeks had passed, at least one thousand souls had accepted Jesus as Savior and Lord, hundreds, if not thousands, had been healed, and many more were filled with the Holy Spirit. Five new churches sprung up to minister to the new converts, with four of them running over two hundred people one year later.

What an honor and joy to be the one young man God would choose to accompany this humble man of God to see this incredible move of God's Spirit on a nation. Again, I can say, this would not have happened if I had chosen to cling to my spiritual pride that evening in our dormitory prayer meeting. Thank God, He convicted me and helped me to humble myself before my peers.

LESSONS IN HUMILITY AS ASSOCIATE PASTOR

After finishing seminary and then working as a house painter for another year in Regina, we journeyed back to Albany, Oregon, to be associate pastors with our beloved Elmer Burnette (or Brother Burnette as everyone called him). We served seven more years under his leadership. Previous to that we had pastored the little country church for five years, and assisted Brother Burnette for one year shortly after our marriage.

Those were great years for learning and growing, but also for God to show me that I still had a great deal more to learn before I was ready for the high calling I felt on my life. Brother Burnette was a kind and gentle man and had a lot of patience with me. He had mentored six other young men before me while he traveled as an evangelist. He had also started six churches, staying long enough to get them established, before turning them over to the Christian and Missionary Alliance leaders in the district. His wife seldom accompanied him, staying home with four children, but he would take a young man or two with him and teach them to pray for the people for salvation, healing or deliverance.

Brenda and I benefited greatly from his past experiences and we dearly loved this man. He did let us know occasionally how we could do things in a better way, but seldom did we feel picked on or judged.

I was still a young radical, teaching everyone about the cost of discipleship and being willing to forsake all and take up their cross to follow Jesus. We felt that the end times were upon us and many of us may be required to suffer for Jesus or even be martyred. I was encouraging other young adults in the church to prepare for persecution and have a place that would be hidden away from government spies, etc. I was also seeing the need for more of a communal lifestyle to save resources and train people for ministry. We talked about pooling our resources to buy some land on the back side of a small mountain in Oregon. I really wanted to go for it and was willing to do what most of the people weren't willing to do. Because I was an ordained preacher and associate pastor, I would get to preach occasionally and had publically shared my passionate beliefs.

At one point, I went a little too far for the older leaders in the church. They complained about my teaching (and long preaching) to Pastor Burnette. He had to try to calm me and them down a little. I felt I was right and stood by my convictions, but did try to use a little more wisdom.

There was truth in most of what I had spoken, but my pride in wanting to be right was an obstacle to my being able to see more clearly and hear what others had to say. I was simply right and they were wrong. I would be patient with them, but eventually, they would see that I was right.

Another situation occurred while under Pastor Burnette's ministry. As the associate pastor of a smaller church, I was in charge when Elmer was away or ill. He was not in good health much of the time and at one point had open heart surgery. I was a part-time commercial painter and part time pastor. When Elmer was sick, I would spend more time at the church office.

There was a sharp young couple in the church and the husband was one of the leaders in the Christian school we started there. While I was alone in the church building, his wife started coming for counseling, regarding her marriage. I was full of confidence that I could help her and her husband have a better marriage. I had two degrees, with a few classes in counseling and I had the Holy Spirit and some experience with deliverance, which I knew was needed in this situation. I was ready to prove to myself and others that I was qualified for the job I had been given.

What my naïve mind did not discern was that she didn't

really want counseling. She wanted to leave her husband for someone who had a higher position. I really thought my wife could help counsel her, but she didn't seem to want that either. Brenda was pregnant at the time and immediately began to pick up on this gal's motives. The short version of the story is that even though there was no physical relationship, my self-confidence and pride in my ability and my anointing led to great hurt and disruption of harmony in both our marriages. Brenda and I and her husband did minister deliverance to her, but she went back to her old ways, caused by insecurity from a lack of affirmation from her father. He had often complimented her sister's beauty, but not hers. Thus, she was always seeking affirmation from others to prove to herself that she was not ugly.

A few years later, we had moved on to pioneer a church in Raymond, Washington. This young couple had been chosen to pastor the church after Brother Burnette's retirement. It wasn't long until she ran off with a visiting musician, leaving the church and her husband in disarray. How different things could had been if I had been more humble and willing to seek more help and wisdom from God and others. But in my youthful desire to prove I was spiritually armed and dangerous, I allowed the enemy to bring pain to my own wife and my friend in ministry, not to mention a whole congregation.

PIONEERING A NEW CHURCH

After serving under Pastor Burnette for a total of eight full years, the Lord clearly told us to move on. We ended up on the southwest coast of Washington in a town called Raymond. That chapter of our life lasted over 14 years.

Finally, I was a senior pastor of a brand new church. We were sent out by a larger church in Aberdeen. There were at least two families that had been driving there every Sunday and they wanted to start a church like Rhema Fellowship in their own town.

Raymond, South Bend and Willapa Valley were three towns with separate school districts in Willapa Harbor. These towns had once thrived because of a huge timber industry and fishing. The decline in these industries had caused a serious decline in population over the previous few decades. Where there had been over thirty different lumber mills there were now only three. Interestingly, there had also been over thirty different taverns in town and that number had also dropped to about three.

I'm not sure how many churches there had been in Willapa Harbor, but probably most of them still existed, although they were just barely surviving. Most of them had less than twenty active members, and the majority of those members were senior citizens. There were a couple of Baptist churches of different stripes and a variety of other traditional denominations and a few independent groups. The two largest churches were a Catholic church with close to 200 members and an Assembly of God church, which had that many at times.

We were being sent out to start a new cutting edge church that had introduced some great new worship songs and a theology of restoration. We believed God was reviving His church and it would once again look like the book of Acts and even better. I still believe that today, but I hope I have a better perspective on it after all these years. The point I want to make is that I was ready to turn this town upside down. I had something fresh to give them, whereas the others were mostly speaking the same things the people had heard all their lives.

In my first ministerial meeting, I sized up the other pastors. I considered them to be mostly weak and old-fashioned. They obviously had little to offer, compared to what I was bringing to Willapa Harbor. I had confidence that we would soon see great things being accomplished in this community.

I was however, naïve enough to believe that the other pastors would like me. I didn't realize that I and the church I represented in Aberdeen were a threat to all these other pastors. The church that sent us out was the fastest growing church in the region. Many people had left their former churches to go to the church where they were getting fed with fresh manna from Heaven. The pastors, whose territory I was invading, were, for the most part, not looking for fresh manna from Heaven. They wanted to keep the people and financial resources they still had and looked on with suspicion any new pastor who could potentially steal some of the few people they had left.

APPARENT SUCCESS

Those were interesting days. If you've ever started a new church, you probably know what kind of people you are going to attract. The solid Christians in the community are already pillars in other churches. There may be a few sincere seekers, who are looking for a move of God, but the majority of your visitors will be those who have not found a church that accepts them. They may be super-critical or very high-maintenance individuals that other churches have given up on.

We found out that there were quite a few of the latter type in the Harbor. But in the early days, things were looking pretty good. We were meeting in the home of one of the main leaders in our brand new congregation, after starting out briefly in the local Grange Hall. The house was packed with families with lots of kids. We had three of our own by then and there were a lot more for them to play with. Pretty soon another small group of believers came to check us out. At one point, we had sixty to seventy people jammed into that home. We felt we were on the way to our goal to transform the community.

The other group visited two or three times and then decided to start their own church a ways out in the country. Others had come and gone. Our numbers dropped quickly as many curiosity seekers found out we were not what they were looking for. Over the course of seven years, we continued to minister a message of revival, holiness and discipleship. Our numbers were fairly steady around thirty or forty people for most of that time.

We also started a Christian School our first year there—a move that some thought unwise. But we were radical believers in Christian education and would not even consider putting our own kids in any public school. At first, we had only one or two other kids in the school, but after several years it had grown to as many as seventy students. We took in many kids that were rejected in the public schools for various reasons. We did our best to introduce them to Jesus and had some success in seeing lives transformed. But the greatest fruit came from kids who had Christian parents and a solid church life. Many later became pastors and church leaders and are serving God today.

One of my ambitious goals was to radically transform many kids in the community and also to even change the political climate. I taught the kids the importance of restoring the Bible and prayer in schools and government institutions. I taught them about the evils of abortion. Some of the kids were really too young to understand and I got in trouble with a one set of parents.

Although I'm sure we influenced a number of people, both students and parents, I was a total failure in accomplishing my dreams to transform the political and moral philosophy of the community. But with eternal optimism, I kept trying until God moved us on to our next assignment.

A TALE OF TWO COUPLES

Shortly after starting Willapa Harbor Christian Fellowship, two different families began coming to the church. They had different backgrounds, but both had much in common. The two major issues were marriage conflicts and a problems in handling their finances. As a young pastor in my late thirties, these two families presented me with a great challenge to prove my counseling wisdom and spiritual gifts.

I was good with math and I felt like I could show these couples how they could get out of debt on their present income. I would help them make a budget and show them how good life could become if they got out of debt. I also felt like I had special wisdom for success in marriage. After all, God had given me a lot of revelation already, including the importance of being humble. I was still naïve enough to believe that I had attained a certain level of humility myself. I didn't realize how much pride I had in my own ability to bring healing to other marriages.

The results of my efforts were less than spectacular, to save the least. Both seemed willing to follow the budget at first, but that lasted only a few days. They had no motivation to discipline themselves to live on a budget. They felt like I was trying to control their lives and they were right. My motivation was as much to prove myself as to help them.

Fixing their marriages was equally unsuccessful. Both couples eventually divorced and both had children who suffered because of the failed marriages. But my self-esteem also took a hit as once again, as I had to deal with the fact that my great gifts and anointings were not as great as I had thought.

As I shared earlier, God had to honor His Word. He said a number of times that He would resist the proud. My pride was keeping me from success. It was God's mercy that He didn't let me succeed in these endeavors and become so proud that He would have to take His hand off of my life and ministry completely.

TO BE PERCEIVED AS A PROPHETIC MAN OF GOD

Being aware that I had a divine calling from childhood and having had some spiritual gifts confirmed early in my life, I was confident that I could predict coming events based on what I felt God was saying to me when I read the Scripture devotionally. I was not analyzing the letter of the "Logos" Word, but rather asking God to speak to me through a "Rhema" Word. I felt that He was saying certain things about our community and they were not all positive.

Like many other young ministers, I was willing for even bad things to happen, if they would prove I was right and had really heard from God. If what I said came true, then people would more readily listen to me. Growing up with two older brothers, I was often treated as the little kid, who didn't know very much compared to them. I had to work hard to get anyone to listen to me and take me seriously. Without realizing the deeper dynamics of my motivation, I was using my spiritual authority and position to reinforce my feeble self-image.

I'm not sure how many of my predictions came to pass, but I know I missed it on some of them. Again, it was God's mercy that kept me from growing more proud and more unusable to God.

A MAJOR SHAKING

After seven years of running the church without any significant administrative skills, while also running the school and working part time, some of my leaders were getting restless and wondering why they were still with me. After seven years, we were down to only three solid families that were tithing members. One day all three got together at our church building to discuss the situation and discover what the others were thinking about it.

I was working, but came home early and stopped by to pick up something from my office. I was surprised to find a meeting going on. A little embarrassed, they asked me to join the conversation and told me what the meeting was about. They confronted me honestly with their concerns. The end result was that all three families left the church at the same time. Some kept sending us at least a part of their tithes for awhile, because they still cared about our family, but we were severely shaken by this blow to our ministry.

It brought me to a new place of brokenness before God. I sought the Lord about whether we were supposed to move on. I tried to find out if there were any other young Bible School grads that might be looking for a challenge. We still had a few people, and a small debt-free building, but no one anywhere was interested. I continued to seek the Lord and He told me to stay. Shortly after that we were given a prophetic word about how the enemy had tried to take us out of the ministry, but God was going to give us strength to go on.

We ended up staying another seven years. God restored my passion for unity through humility. Pastors began to get together for prayer. We were no longer a threat to them as people who had come from their churches to us had now returned to them or moved on somewhere else. In addition, God brought us people who were Hispanic. I loved the Spanish language and anyone who spoke it because it brought back the great memories of my six weeks in Argentina. Soon we had a second congregation with Spanish services every Sunday.

At the same time more people were coming to the English services and God was moving in our midst. The humbling of that church split had done more for me than steady growth could have done. I knew how much I needed God and how merciful He had been to me.

LIVING DEBT FREE—OR NOT?

I inherited a tendency to be radical. My parents were willing to be different if they thought it would please God. They believed in Jesus as their healer and would not go to a doctor. I was born at home in the cabin my father had built. He was the only one assisting my mother when she gave birth to my brother and me. I like to tell people he had a deliverance ministry. I was about seventeen before I went to a doctor or hospital. By this time, my parents had moderated their convictions somewhat and my ingrown toenail needed attention.

I mention the above to make it clear that I inherited some

tendencies to be radical with my convictions. One of these was to stay out of debt. Although we had very little income at times, when we depended on the church and Christian school to provide our needs, we had managed to get and stay out of debt. I was debt free and took pride in that. I felt that others could do the same if they had the faith and the conviction not to borrow.

Once again, the Lord showed me that my pride was worse than debt and He began to allow things to happen. Our daughter fell out of a tree and broke a bone in her arm. We had to take her to the doctor, not having money or insurance. All of a sudden we had some debt we had no way to avoid. Soon dental emergencies arose and we had some dentist bills. After that we had to travel to Mexico, then to our son's wedding in Wisconsin. We had to have credit cards to rent cars, etc., so we gave in to that, since we already had medical bills.

Soon we had several thousand dollars worth of debt and our boasting about being debt free had come to an end. When God led us into a travelling ministry, we used personal and ministry credit cards to get from place to place and God provided income and supporters to make the payments, but before long the economy tanked and supporters dropped us and we were in trouble. We had to humble ourselves and apply for credit counseling relief. God helped us to pay off tens of thousands of dollars of debt over a four year period while the economy was still very bad. We still have to trust God for monthly income to make our mortgage and utility payments and payments on our vehicles.

Once again, my spiritual pride had robbed me of God's favor for a time. He allowed me to be humbled so He could offer extra grace to me for the important days in which we now live and the days of harvest which are still coming.

Chapter Four

Pride and Its Accomplices

A very long time ago, God made men and women in His own image. We still have the DNA of God in our soul and spirit. Satan hates God and he hates us because we were made in the image of God. He had so much power and glory in Heaven, but he was not made in the image of God and we were. Wanting to hurt God and usurp His power, Satan determined to make us into his own image as much as possible.

Pride was the source of Satan's rebellion. It was now at the heart of his perverted nature. It was Eve's pride that he appealed to and through it he was able to sow the seeds of pride to all future children of Eve. I believe that this pride has been passed on from generation to generation in an unbroken chain. We were all born with this disease and only God's intervention through the power of the Holy Spirit can give us the strength to resist pride and humble ourselves before God and others.

WE ALL SUFFER WITH "I" TROUBLE

This only works in English, but the middle letter—the heart of the word - "PRIDE" is "I". Similarly, the middle letter of the word "SIN" is "I". The "I" in us is the driving force that causes so many problems in our lives.

I believe the root of all sin is the "I" in us that is the heart of pride, which as we said before, God must resist in order to be faithful to His Word. Yes, the love of money is a root of all kinds of evil (meaning bad things happening), but it is not THE root of all sin (see I Timothy 6:10 NKJV).

The love of money is itself rooted in pride. We love money mostly because of what it can do for us in gaining us honor and pleasure. The love of money causes lots of problems for people. Many are in prison or dead because of it. Thieves and drug dealers, mafia and too many politicians have become casualties of the love of money. But clearly, most of them loved the power and pleasure—some of pride's associates—that money brought them.

So let's see if we can learn how to solve our "I" problems. Perhaps we will actually see more clearly as we discover how subtle our enemy is in enticing us into the place where God actually has to resist us instead of helping us.

DEFINING AND UNDERSTANDING PRIDE

We haven't yet clearly defined humility, but perhaps we will get a better idea about humility if we have a better understanding of what pride really is. I don't believe most of us really understand pride and how many forms and subtleties it can manifest through. We usually think in terms of pride being just thinking you are important or special, etc.

My own personal definition of pride is as follows:

Pride is a force within our soul, also called "ego", that is always trying to elevate us (especially in the eyes of others) and that same force is always trying to prevent us from being put down (especially in the eyes of others).

*In other words, **pride is an upward force or push and a resistance to any downward force or push within our soul.***

This upward push and resistance to any downward push is at work in our lives when we are born and kicks into high gear as soon as we discover positive and negative input into our soul. When the people in our little world show us positive attention and praise, we feel uplifted, but when anger is directed towards us for our crying or mess-making, we feel a desire to prevent the downward push on our soul.

Toddlers love to show off every little way they can when they get positive attention from others. But if they don't feel safe or secure in the presence of certain people, they will try to hide behind a parent or sibling, fearing they will be put down or embarrassed. They may also throw a little fit if something is taken from them and their perceived rights are violated.

By school age the child loves the praise of the teacher and the honor and admiration of others. Children will also hide from attention if they have been hurt in the past. It is the same basic inner force that causes one child to show off and another child to hide from the public eye.

We are not being humble when we are acting shy or staying out of sight. We are simply expressing pride in a different way.

PRIDE'S MULTIPLE MANIFESTATIONS

1. SHOWING OFF, BOASTING, ETC.

These are the obvious manifestations of pride. No need to amplify.

2. SHYNESS, INSECURITY, ETC.

These are some of the more subtle ways pride manifests as mentioned above. Insecurity results from the fear of being pushed down and kept from the security of being accepted, affirmed and loved. Fear of public speaking is a top ranking phobia, because when everyone is looking at us, we are afraid of what they are thinking of us. They are probably being critical, and we don't want to be put down in their eyes.

3. ANGER

You wouldn't normally think of anger as a manifestation of pride, but it truly is. Anger is a feeling that your rights were taken away and that someone has pushed downward on your soul, making you less than you are. For example, if your child back-talks to you, you might get angry and say or think, "Who do you think you are? Do you know who you're talking to? I could ground you for a month or slap you silly." You would be feeling like you were not getting the honor you deserve. Your child is pushing down on your own ego and place of honor. The only reason you get angry is you feel put down.

If you hit your thumb nail instead of the construction nail with a hammer, you might yell or cuss in anger. What made you angry? It wasn't just the pain. You felt violated by the "stupid" hammer. You are a better carpenter than that. You are being deprived of progress and you are being made to feel "stupid," even if no one is around. And through it all, you feel you have a right not to have that pain. You don't deserve it. Your well being is being taken from you. You are being robbed of your rights.

If someone else flirts with your "special someone," you could easily become very angry at that person. That "special someone" makes you feel important and secure in your soul when they bless you with their favor. The other person is a threat to your soulish security and wellbeing. They could make you feel less important and less loved and therefore more insecure. It makes you angry because someone else is taking what you need for your own ego support.

4. JEALOUSY

The previous example shows how jealousy and anger work together in a "deadly duo" combination. How many violent crimes have resulted from jealous lovers? As we illustrated above, jealousy comes from a fear of personal loss of honor, love and affirmation. All of these are rooted in pride—the ego force within our soul.

5. SELF-PITY

What a nasty one this is! And it is also rooted in the ego force called pride. We feel sorry for ourselves because we have been put down and not exalted as we truly deserve. "Nobody likes me, everybody hates me, I'm going to the garden to eat worms."

Pity parties are such carnal pacifiers for our egos. Often they lead to both anger and the next items on our list below. The reason it leads to these damaging actions is that when we agree with the lie that nobody loves us, we open ourselves up to a "spirit of agreement" with the enemy.

The spirit of agreement makes it easier for us to believe other lies that we would normally reject, such as how we should hurt someone so they will feel pain like they caused us to feel. This manifestation of pride has caused an incredible amount of pain to multitudes of people, including millions of Christians.

6. REVENGE

If someone has hurt me and I feel sorry for myself, I may also believe the lie that I should look for a special way to get revenge. The other person put me down and made me feel stupid or bad, so now it's my turn to get even. They will be sorry for what they did to me when I get through with them. The ultimate revenge is:

7. SUICIDE

Yes, suicide is usually the ultimate revenge for someone who has been hurt. They know the person will never be able to ask and receive forgiveness. They can put them in a prison of guilt for the rest of their lives. Who could ask for better revenge? And it all stems from the ego wanting to be honored and affirmed by other people. The idea is now believable because we have come into a spirit of agreement with the enemy when we agreed with the lie that no one really loves us.

8. LYING

Almost all lying is motivated by wanting to look good, or by not wanting to look bad. We don't want to feel the shame or else we want to be honored and admired by others. Lance Armstrong finally admitted he had lied over and over again, because he had such a strong desire to keep his reputation as the top cyclist in the world. It was an inflated ego and it has brought a huge amount of pain to himself and many others.

9. FEAR

Why do we fear? Mostly, we fear loss of possessions, position, power and the respect of others. We fear our natural source of security will be taken away, leaving us vulnerable to be put down and hurt. Those who possess the most of the above have the greatest problems with fear, because they have more to lose. But there is no greater fear for most people than the fear of being put down by others.

10. IMMORAL BEHAVIOR

While immoral behavior is often a giving in to fleshly and hormonal desires, the human ego is often involved. Some men and women may feel they can handle a little extra non-acceptable sexual stimulation without getting into trouble. Whether it's pornography or flirting, it gratifies the flesh and is justified by self-confidence.

A dear personal friend is now evangelizing and making disciples of Jesus on the inside of a state prison, because, as a prison guard, he had gotten careless and cocky and allowed a female inmate to entice him to do what was not legal or moral to do. He learned quickly that God resists the proud but gives grace to the humble.

IMPORTANT CLARIFICATION

God wants us to have a healthy self-image, and He understands where we come from and what we have been through. He knows that we are born insecure and are predisposed to try to try to promote ourselves to gain people's favor. So He offers His hand of grace to help us overcome our many handicaps and bad habits. Jesus went to the cross to pay the price of victory over every inherited weakness and every strategy of the enemy of our souls.

He knows that we are all born with a need for affirmation and love. In a perfect world, that would come in big doses from our parents and extended family. They, in turn, would teach us how to receive the love and affirmation of our Heavenly Father, so that we do not depend on the world for love and affirmation. The enemy would have a lot less opportunity to take advantage of the heightened insecurity that most children grow up with today.

But of course, this is a far from perfect world and we grow up feeling a great lack of affirmation and love. If we don't have a strong intimate relationship with God, we continuously look for security in all the wrong places. It becomes the normal thing to do and we don't usually have a clue as to what's going on or why we do or say what we do. And most of what we do to get love and affirmation backfires on us and we feel less love and less affirmed than ever.

God truly understands and offers us His grace the moment we humble ourselves and ask for His help and forgiveness. However, if we harden our hearts and blame others and don't forgive them, we are actually asking God to resist us and not forgive our own sins.

PRIDE AND SOME SYNONYUMS IN SCRIPTURE

Using Strong's Concordance and the King James Version, I found the following words and the number of their occurrences in Scripture. They are always treated as evil and open for correction or judgment.

pride, proud, proudly:	*106x*
haughty	*10x*
scorner	*15x*
arrogancy	*4x*
vain	*25x*
conceit	*8x*

SOME NASTY CONSEQUENCES OF PRIDE

Proverbs 13:10 says that pride results in strife or contention.

Proverbs 16:18 says that pride precedes destruction and a haughty spirit precedes a fall.

Proverbs 29:23 says a man's pride will bring him low.

Isaiah 9:9 talks about a people who refuse correction because of pride and arrogance. God promises to bring utter destruction upon them.

Mathew 23:12. Jesus said that "Whoever exalts himself will be humbled."

Luke 1:51 says that God scatters the proud.

Both James 4:6 and I Peter 5:5 tell us that God resists the proud.

There are so many more, but this sample should make the point. There are also many stories and historical comments about kings and leaders who were deposed because of pride. Certainly, the story of King Saul is a prime example. While he was losing favor with God because of disobedience, he actually set up a monument for himself.

Then in fear and jealousy and anger—all symptoms of pride—he chased David around the country. In doing this, Saul lost his best warrior, who had never lost a battle, and opened the country to attack on the west coast while he was chasing David on the east coast of Israel, by the Dead Sea. Ultimately, he lost his life in a war that David should have fought and won for him. Truly, his pride preceded his destruction.

IS THERE A "GOOD" PRIDE??

We frequently use the expression, "I'm so proud of you!" or "I'm so proud to be an American." Is it wrong to say these things in the light of the fact that God hates pride and resists it?

In my younger and more idealistic days, I campaigned against such statements, declaring that God hates all pride and we confuse our children when we use a word that means something bad all throughout Scripture to mean something good. I taught people to use different words like, "I'm so pleased with you!" or "I'm so thankful to be an American."

Today, I chose my battles more carefully. I do have more important assignments on my life than semantics. I know what people mean when they use the word, "proud." God does look at the heart. He doesn't resist us because we say we're proud of someone, but He will resist us if we are proud of the fact that we don't use that word the wrong way.

While it would seem to be better to change our vocabulary and teach children the meaning of pride and humility, it's so much more important that we demonstrate humility and teach them by example. Children, like all of us, are attracted to humility and turned off by pride.

Chapter Five

Understanding Humility

Now that we've looked at pride and its accomplices, let's look more deeply into what humility is and how we can develop this valuable, but elusive entity. I shared earlier how great a blessing one act of humility was to my life. I've also shared how destructive my pride has been on the ministry journey. In this chapter, we will try to put together a tool kit to kill pride and feed our desire to be like Jesus, who humbled Himself to provide eternal life for all who would come to Him.

DEFINING THE TERM

We established earlier that humility was not me putting myself down. That is just another manifestation of pride, because it is focused on me. When I publically put myself down, I'm usually looking for someone to say, "Hey, you're not so bad."

Whereas the essence of pride is focus on self and the need to exalt the ego, the essence of humility is focusing on others and making them feel loved and affirmed. It is looking past our own need for love and affirmation, and giving it to others, because we've gotten all the love and affirmation that we need from our loving Heavenly Father.

> *Humility is:* **An attitude of gratitude to God and others for all they have done to bless my life. It is a desire to give, serve and put others first, like Jesus did. It is nt a downward self-deprecating force, but an upward force that focuses on lifting others rather than self.**
>
> *Humility is actually seeing ourselves as we really are in the light of God's glory and His grace. We recognize the ugliness of our sinful hearts, but at the same time we experience the amazing grace that makes us not only accepted, but actually sons and daughters and joint heirs with the very Son of God.*

SOME OF THE BLESSINGS OF HUMILITY

Again, we can only give a small sample. Anyone who so desires can do a complete study on the subject with a good concordance.

1. RESTORATION AND REVIVAL

Second Chronicles 7:14 is one of the best-known verses on revival and restoration. It begins by saying, "If My people, who are called by My name, will humble themselves . . ." Humbling ourselves is the first thing required, followed by prayer, seeking God's face and turning from our wicked ways. The promise to those who do those things is that God will hear us in Heaven, forgive our sins and heal our land. Those are great promises to those who first humble themselves and then follow through with the other three requirements. When God heals our land, it means reformation of the whole society and the productivity of the soil, etc. It can mean the end of drought, pestilences and natural disasters that come when our society turns away from God.

2. LIVING IN GOD'S PRESENCE

Isaiah 57:15 is one of my favorites. It goes like this:

"For thus says the High and Lofty One, Who inhabits eternity, whose name is Holy, 'I dwell in the high and holy place, with him who has a contrite and humble spirit, to revive the spirit of the humble, and to revive the heart of the contrite ones.'" (NKJV).

Could anyone ask for any greater reward than to actually live in close relationship with the Creator and the King of the Universe? He promises to dwell with us when we are humble and contrite, bringing us up into His high and holy place where He lives.

3. HONOR AND EXALTATION

The same passages that tell us that God resists the proud tell us that He exalts the humble. In other words, when you seek things for your own selfish purposes, you will lose it all. When you seek first His Kingdom and His righteousness, you get what the others are seeking. Amazing, isn't it?

4. GRACE

James and Peter both told us that God resists the proud, but gives grace to the humble. What does that mean to us today? How important is grace? Is it just a theological term or does it make a difference in our lives?

Without grace, we have nothing at all. Everything of value comes through God's grace. If you like God's spiritual gifts, they come from God's grace. The word "grace" is "karis" in the Greek. The word "gift" is "karisma" in the Greek. In other words, the word for grace is contained in the word for gift. A gift is thus a "thing of grace."

But think of it now in different terms. Someone you love is dying with cancer. Without a miracle you will lose a dear friend. You need a miracle which only comes from God's grace—His undeserved favor and power to see the impossible made possible.

While there are many different factors involved in why some people are healed and others aren't, one clear factor, according to Scripture, is the pride/humility issue. And this is one thing we do have control of.

We don't have to be super spiritual, wealthy, intelligent, or credentialed to humble ourselves. We just have to humble ourselves. It's very simple, but definitely not very easy.

HUMILITY AND ALLIES IN SCRIPTURE

humble, humility, humble	*60x*
meek, meekness	*31x*
contrite, lowliness, etc.	*12x*

As you can clearly see, pride and humility are common themes in Scripture. With wonderful promises to all who pursue humility, we can see the importance of this one prerequisite for all of God's greatest blessings.

Just as the words "pride" and its companions mentioned in the last chapter are always treated in a negative way, humility and meekness are always treated in a very positive way.

NOTHING GETS MORE RESULTS AND REWARDS THAN HUMILITY

After sixty years of studying Scripture and preaching the gospel, I believe I can say without hesitation (and hopefully, not too much pride) that there is no character quality more important or rewarding for us to seek after than humility. There is no other virtue that God requires from us in order for us to obtain His grace. There is no simpler prescription for being exalted than to humble ourselves. There is no other way to get close to God and live in His high and holy place with Him than to have a meek and humble spirit.

Humility is not only our most valuable asset, but it is still one of the best kept secrets in the Kingdom, partly because talking about it brings unwelcome scrutiny. So what can be done to change all that? We will try to give you some keys and creative ideas in the following chapter.

Chapter Six

Pursuing Humility

KEEPING YOUR EYES ON THE PRIZE

Before we get into the practical ways we can pursue humility, we should take a moment to reinforce our determination to follow through in this pursuit. Your flesh will fight you every step of the way and you may feel like it's too hard and want to give in to your natural instincts, but don't do it! The rewards are so far greater than the price you will pay.

What are the rewards? Let's remind ourselves again.

1. GOD EXTENDS HIS GRACE TO THE HUMBLE.

I believe every little act of humility releases an extra dose of grace for whatever you're going through.

That grace also releases an anointing on your spiritual gifts. Remember gifts come by God's grace.

2. GOD DWELLS IN A HIGH AND HOLD PLACE WITH THOSE WHO HAVE A HUMBLE AND CONTRITE HEART.

Being close and intimate with God should be high on our priority list.

3. GOD EXALTS THE HUMBLE AND PUTS DOWN THE PROUD.

Those who don't seek to be exalted get exalted. God can trust the humble with a high place. He is looking for those He can exalt for the sake of His Kingdom. Those with high positions can influence and impact the society and the nation. It's sad that He finds so few in the Kingdom that He can trust with high position. The result is that evil men rise to the top through wicked strategies and destroy the moral culture of the society they exploit.

4. HUMILITY IS THE FIRST STEP IN BRINGING REVIVAL AND RESTORATION OF OUR SOCIETY.

This doesn't happen overnight, but it has to start somewhere with someone. Why not let that someone be us and the somewhere be right where we live? This is certainly a great reason to learn to practice humility. It's not only something we desperately need, but it's also something God's heart longs for.

SEIZING THE MOMENT

Learning humility is not something you can put on your calendar like a college course. You don't get a one hour a day class from 9:00 AM till 10:00 AM. Opportunities to learn and practice humility can come without warning at the least expected moment. Thus, we must learn to discipline ourselves to watch for these opportunities and seize the moment when they spring up out of nowhere.

These moments usually happen when something negative, like criticism against us occurs. Our normal response is to get into a "fight" mode. Self-defense is instinctive—humbling ourselves is not. In other words, to seize the moment requires going against our natural instinct. That instinct is programmed into our psyche and does not easily get erased. It requires an alert and vigilant mind and heart to identify and overrule it.

Other opportunities to practice humbling ourselves come when we are honored or complimented. Many sports reporters, who interview the star of the game, lead with a compliment, noting the great accomplishments of the athlete. It opens the door for the player to talk about himself. However, most of these accomplished athletes have also been trained how to respond to such interviews. You will notice that they always deflect the praise and talk about the team and the coach, etc., not taking the credit they rightly could. Whether they truly feel that way, they know what makes them look good and what would make them look bad.

True humility is giving God and others the credit and the glory from our heart of hearts, not just our mouth. It requires stirring up a spirit of thanksgiving and honor. It doesn't come natural, but with practice it becomes much easier.

GETTING HEALED OF INNER PAIN

None of us grew up in a totally perfect environment. Even those of us who grew up in God-fearing homes experienced a certain amount of rejection, loss, criticism, judgment and guilt. Negative experiences had an effect on our sense of self-worth and security. Fear of a repetition of the pain affected our personalities and we became more cautious and timid or rebellious and overly bold.

The end result is that we become less secure about whom we are and our pride and ego are wounded. Like a wounded and cornered wild animal, we are ready for a fight or on the other hand, we may have given up hope and gone into self-pity or depression. In either of these conditions we find it very difficult to humble ourselves.

The solution for this is to get healed in our soul. Inner healing is once again a major focus in the church and the Kingdom of God. There are many different forms and philosophies of inner healing, but the goal is the same. God wants people to be free of their inner pain so they can be free to fulfill their destiny without being shipwrecked by a sudden storm of emotions.

Inner healing involves identifying sources of previous pain and forgiving those who caused the pain. It also involves breaking negative ties with previous generations and breaking off generational curses. One of the pioneer inner healing ministries is called Elijah House Ministries, founded by John and Paula Sandford in 1975. Some more recent versions of inner healing have used the term, "Sozo," which is a Greek word for "life". Many other forms exist, some of which may be a bit controversial, but all of them are designed to bring healing to the heart and soul of people who have been wounded by life.

For the topic of this book, inner healing is a key to being able to develop a humble heart. However, one should be warned that the process itself usually requires a significant amount of humbling. Sharing your past pain with someone else is not usually easy. Even "tough guys" often break down as they relive their past painful encounters.

The reward of getting your soul healed is that many sources of insecurity are dealt with and when you are more secure in who you are, it is much easier to think of others and express true humility. People who are insecure find it hard to think about others, because they are so self-conscious, wondering what other people are thinking of them.

Although inner healing is not a one-time cure, once you have learned the process, you can deal with pain as it happens and live a life-style of inner healing. This process is such a wonderful companion to the process of learning to humble ourselves. Each process enables us to do the other easier and better.

PRIME OPPORTUNITIES TO PRACTICE HUMBLING OURSELVES

1. MARRIAGE

If you are married, you have already discovered that there are no shortages of opportunities to practice humbling yourselves on a daily basis. Marriage is an arrangement God gave us in order for us to see ourselves in a clearer light. It proves that God has a real sense of humor in how He made us. Most of us were attracted to our mates, for the most part, because of what we saw when we looked at them. But when we began to live together in close quarters, we found out that they were really mirrors, revealing what we looked like in ways we didn't always appreciate.

Both men and women have egos and pride. Men express or reveal it mostly as it relates to their achievements, while women express or reveal it mostly as it relates to their human relationships and physical appearance.

I won't share any personal examples here, but God knew whom He needed to put in my life—someone with a totally different background—someone who did not have the religious pride that I had grown up with. She also has a gift of discerning of spirits that makes her uncomfortable when my religious spirit manifests.

HOW HARD IS IT TO SAY, "I WAS WRONG?"

For some reason, many married people find it extremely difficult to say, "I'm sorry, I was wrong. Please forgive me!" But if we really want to pursue the blessings and favor God gives to the humble, we should jump at the opportunity whenever it presents itself.

Many times the Lord has reminded me that the wife He gave me is also His daughter and His bride. He wants me to treat her with respect because He is watching over her to make sure she is treated well. I'd rather humble myself and ask for forgiveness for my attitude than fight for my rights and offend God for the way I am treating His daughter and His bride.

2. CHILDREN AND PARENT

We will address how to practice humbling ourselves on a regular basis with children and parents, but first I want to address parents who are struggling with children who have already closed their spirits to one or both of them.

If you are a parent of growing children, you will often find yourself stressed by their behavior. I'm pretty sure that from time to time, we have all responded out of our flesh—our pride—and said degrading things or displayed a negative spirit on our countenances when we talked with them. We probably felt justified, thinking that they deserved it because of their disobedience or lack of respect, etc.

But every time we talked down to them or demonstrated anger without apologizing, we took away some of their own self-worth, causing their own pride to react to ours. Some children are more sensitive than others and don't require a lot of negative input before they respond by rebellion or by withdrawing into their shell.

Either way, they have closed their spirit to us and we have our work cut out to reopen it again. The GOOD NEWS is that in most cases it can be done and I have personally seen it happen with my own children.

Here is my best advice to any parent who has lost the heart of one or more of their children, and this is especially for fathers, and especially those who say, I've done everything possible to make them happy and nothing has worked. The problem usually is that we really haven't done everything possible. Please try the following prescription for restoring your kids.

A. Ask God for forgiveness for offending and causing one of His own children to stumble. If you gave your life to God, you probably also gave your children to Him. They are His kids regardless. He created them and fashioned them in the womb. He died for them and loves them even more than you do. They are loaned to you and you are to be good stewards of His resources. Imagine how you would feel if you let another family watch your kids while you were away and you found out the other family had treated them in anger and emotionally abused them. How does God feel when we emotionally abuse His children, even when we think they deserved it because of their behavior.

B. Commit yourself to communicating in a way that will show respect and love. Ask them to give you an opportunity to listen to them—not to talk to them. You may want to write a note or send a text that they can think about in private before responding. Try to make an appointment and give them an assignment. Ask them to prepare for your time with them by listing the various times that you hurt or embarrassed them or failed to keep a promise you made to them.

Tell them that you promise not to excuse or defend yourself or explain why you did what you did. You just want to hear what is on their heart so you can feel their pain and apologize for it. You can start out by telling them that God has convicted you about the way you have treated them or talked to them in the past.

Disclaimer: This doesn't mean that you relinquish your responsibilities as a father or mother, especially if they still have a lot of growing up to do. It simply means that for this appointment, you will listen to their hearts and take all the blame you can so they feel listened to and loved. You can later reaffirm your standards and rules in your home, but you will do it with a lot more love and grace.

C. Follow through and make sure the appointment happens. Reaffirm your purpose and promise to just listen and not argue or justify yourself. No matter how skewed the accusations seem, realize that this is how they have perceived things from their own perspective.

D. Ask God to help you feel their pain and see things from their viewpoint. Ask Him to give you compassion and grace to overlook any exaggeration or false accusation. Your words are not enough here. You must really feel their pain and feel sorry about it. They can discern hypocrisy quickly and have probably been programmed to expect it. They may have a hard time believing you will really follow through with this plan.

E. Make a thorough apology and ask for their forgiveness. If they allow it, give them an extended hug and tell them how much you love and appreciate them. Speak and prophesy destiny into their lives. Tell them how much God cares and how special they are in His Kingdom and in your own heart. Tell them you want to be the best father any kid ever had and that you want their help to know how to accomplish that.

My guess is that if you truly follow this prescription, your child will be broken up just like you and you will shed a few tears on each other's shoulders. It could be one of the best and happiest days of your life.

ONGOING OPPORTUNITIES FOR PARENTS TO HUMBLE THEMSELVES

While the above five point prescription was to restore a child who has hardened his or her heart to a parent, we want to now address the normal day-to-day opportunities to humble ourselves with our children. If we follow these suggestions, we should greatly reduce the risk that we will ever lose their hearts.

1. Ask God to make you more sensitive to the way you communicate with your children. Each one is different and different things will offend them. We need God's help.
2. Give your spouse and other children permission to tell you if they think you are saying or doing something that could offend or wound their spirit. Many times God won't speak directly to us if we're too proud to listen to those He has put in our lives. Remember: God resists the proud, but gives grace to the humble.
3. Apologize quickly. Don't wait to cool off. Take the blame and ask for forgiveness. Say, "I was wrong in talking to you like that. You are a very special child of God and I had no right to treat you with disrespect. Please forgive me! I'm asking God to help me not to talk to you like that. Please pray for me! I want to be the best parent a child ever had. Please help me to be that.

I believe you will be very blessed by the results of this humility. Remember most people resist the proud just like God does. But they are drawn to humility and will love you more than ever.

Your greatest reward, however, is not that your children will love and listen to you. Your greatest reward is that God will draw near to you and show you more of His heart and His mind. He will extend His grace to you and give you precious encounters with Him and His Holy Spirit. It is truly a win/win situation for everyone but the thief who comes to steal, kill and destroy. Our enemy will have lost his chance to destroy another family and bring strife and chaos into the homes of the children of the King of Kings.

OPPORTUNITIES FOR CHILDREN

If you are the child (younger or older) with parents whom you are trying to get along with, here are some suggestions for practicing humility with them:

1. Ask God for grace and the power to truly forgive your parents for their mistakes and bad attitudes towards you. Then ask Him to forgive you for any disobedience or rebellion or bad attitudes you have had towards them, including unforgiveness.
2. Thank them often for all they do for you and give to you. They often feel their kids don't appreciate the sacrifices they have made for them. When they hear you thank them, they will be more inclined to bless you even more—but don't let that be your motive. Thankfulness is an essential fruit of true humility.
3. Try to be the first to apologize when you've had an argument or bad attitudes. When you feel anger or resentment, recognize that you are lacking love and need God's grace.

Apologize and ask forgiveness immediately, while you ask God for grace to feel what He feels, rather than what the flesh feels.

4. Offer to do things for your parents that will make their load lighter. Serving is another fruit of true humility. Offering your services is an act of humbling yourself to be their servant. Your natural instinct is to want to be your own grown-up boss and not have to submit to others who don't seem to respect the fact that you are not a little kid anymore.

I can't guarantee that your life will be perfect if you follow this advice, but I'd sure be willing to bet that it will get a lot better.

OTHER OPPORTUNITIES TO PRACTICE HUMILITY

It doesn't matter where we work, study or play, if there are people around, there are opportunities to practice humbling ourselves. I would encourage you to ask God every day for grace to humble yourself throughout the day whenever God gives you the opportunity.

1. Be a servant whenever possible to others, including those below you in the pecking order. Serving is truly a bi-product of humility and will increase your favor with God and man.
2. Take as much of the blame as you can when things go wrong. Don't point the finger at others or feel sorry for yourself if you get blamed. Volunteer to help clean up any mess created and do it with a joyful heart.

3. Express thanks to everyone who has served you or support-
ed you in any way. Give special gifts when they aren't expected to people who need encouragement or appreciation.
4. Forgive others who offend you and ask God for grace to
convince your heart that you really do forgive them.
5. At the end of the day, pause to thank God for the grace He
gave you to humble yourself and also confess where you
may have missed the mark. Ask for forgiveness and grace
to humble yourself more the next day.

Disclaimer: I am in no way suggesting that any of us
submit ourselves to physical or emotional abuse or to
becoming someone's doormat on a regular basis. Humility involves knowing who we are and being secure
in serving others, but it does not mean we facilitate
others in their evil ways. Humility is almost synony-
mous with love. When we love someone, we want to
help them to change. There are times when we need to
show tough love, but we must be careful not to take the
temptation to feel superior or more spiritual. We need
to remember Paul's exhortation to restore others in a
spirit of meekness (Galatians 6:1)

We can't provide hard and fast rules for when we should
tolerate bad behavior and when we should speak out. Jesus accepted a lot of abuse, but He resisted his abusers at other times.
Paul also refused to let the enemy walk all over him on certain
occasions, but he also suffered many persecutions for Christ.

The good news is that if we have learned to humble ourselves before God and others, God walks in close fellowship

with us. He gives us His Holy Spirit to teach us and guide us in each situation. If we ask Him, He will speak to us and we will make the right decision. Like Jesus, we can do what we see the Father doing and say what He is saying.

Chapter Seven

Staying Humble About Our Humility

As is implied in the title of this book, we can get closer and closer to our goal of becoming truly humble, but being able to say we've finally arrived at being perfectly humble is not ever going to happen. But as I shared in my own testimony, it becomes very easy to feel good about ourselves and feel we have arrived, especially when we compare ourselves to others who manifest an abundance of pride.

Pride is one of the most devious entities in our lives. It sneaks up on us when we are least expecting it. It comes disguised as a friend that wants to make us feel good about ourselves. It is difficult to distinguish it sometimes from healthy self-respect. But it is certainly not the same thing.

Healthy self-respect is the acknowledgment that God has lifted us up out of the pit of sin and self, and because of His amazing love and grace, He has made us royalty—sons and daughters of the King of Kings. He has even made us to rule as kings under Him. This is explained in greater detail in my book, "Kings and Kingdoms."

Pride is different. Pride forgets about God's grace and how much He has done for us. Pride focuses on how much we ourselves have accomplished through our talents, skills and hard work. It does not transfer the praise and glory to God.

A KING OF KINGS LEARNS HUMILITY

Remember the story of Nebuchadnezzar, a king of kings, emperor of the nations in Daniel's day. Nebuchadnezzar had been exposed to God's power and majesty. He had witnessed the three Hebrews surviving his fiery furnace without harm. He had made a decree that anyone who spoke evil of their God would be killed, declaring, "There is no other god who is able to deliver after this sort." (Daniel 3:29).

Later he had a dream that Daniel interpreted for him describing a judgment that would come upon him if he didn't humble himself. Daniel concludes his exhortation to Nebuchadnezzar with the following words:

> *"Therefore, O king, let my counsel be acceptable to you, and break off your sins by righteousness, and your iniquities by showing mercy to the poor; if there may be a lengthening of your tranquility." All this came on the king Nebuchadnezzar. At the end of twelve months he was walking in the royal palace of Babylon. The king spoke and said, "Is not this great Babylon, which I have built for the royal*

*dwelling place, by the might of my power and for the glory
of my majesty?" (Daniel 4:27-30 WEB).*

A humble king would have looked at Babylon and felt
overwhelmed by God's goodness in allowing him the privilege
of being king over such a beautiful city. He would have given
thanks and praise to God. But Nebuchadnezzar was lifted up
in pride and the next thing that happened was that he was
struck with insanity and became like a wild animal, eating grass
and was totally out of his right mind.

Nebuchadnezzar obviously hadn't read the Scripture that
God resists the proud but gives grace to the humble. However, when seven years had past, God restored his mind and his
kingdom to him. He then praised and glorified God. Here are
the final words of his own testimony:

> *"Now I, Nebuchadnezzar, praise and extol and honor the
> King of Heaven, all of whose works are truth, and His
> ways justice.* ***And those who walk in pride He is able
> to put down.****" (Daniel 4:37)*

The greatest earthly king, a true king of kings or emperor,
learned a valuable lesson and proclaimed it to all. He was restored as a very humble king.

As I shared earlier, although I had taken a step of humility
and was greatly rewarded by God for it, I still had a heart that
was open to proud thoughts and deeds. We never arrive in this
quest and we never are immune to the deceptions of the enemy.

PETER TAKES A HEALTHY HIT

Consider also Peter, Jesus' most outgoing disciple. He and the other eleven disciples were in the boat when Jesus came walking on the water. At Peter's request, Jesus invited him to walk on the water with Him. Peter was not known for his humility at the time, but his boldness and passion were commendable. He was granted a miracle by Jesus, who knew exactly what was going to happen.

While Peter kept his eyes on Jesus, he had his miracle as Jesus was authoring his faith (Hebrews 12:2). But then he saw the waves approaching. Now let me use my imagination to suggest how this might have happened. I'm guessing that Peter was feeling pretty pleased with himself and I'm sure he was wondering what the other disciples were thinking about him. I don't know if you can relate, but I certainly can. Peter wondered if they were watching him and what they were saying to each other. Surely, they must be pretty impressed with him and his faith, etc.

But as Peter began to turn his head to see if they were watching him, he saw a ten foot wave headed right towards him. Without having his eyes on Jesus, the author and finisher of our faith, Peter was missing the "finisher" part. He soon learned that pride was a snare of the enemy to keep him from a "finished" miracle. As he humbled himself, crying out for help, Jesus lifted him up, just as the Bible declares. He puts down the proud, but lifts up the humble.

REMEMBER HOW JESUS SET THE EXAMPLE FOR US

In Philippians 2:5-11, Paul describes in beautiful language how Jesus gave up His rights to be with His Father in Heaven, in order to come to earth to provide salvation for all who would receive it. Here is what Paul wrote:

> *"Let this mind be in you which was also in Christ Jesus, who, being in the form of God did not consider it robbery to be equal with God, but made Himself of no reputation, taking the form of a bondservant, and coming in the likeness of men. And being found in appearance as a man, He humbled Himself and became obedient to the point of death, even the death of the cross.*
>
> *Wherefore, God also has highly exalted Him and given Him the name which is above every name, that at the name of Jesus every knee should bow of those in Heaven and of those on earth, and of those under the earth, and that every tongue should confess that Jesus Christ is Lord, to the glory of God the Father."*

1. We are exhorted to have the same mind or attitude as Jesus. We can't die for everyone's sins like He did, but we can have the same attitude. What was His attitude? It's very clear from this passage, that His attitude was humility. He left the wealth of Heaven to become a human being who was falsely condemned to die the most cruel and humiliating death known to man. He wasn't just humble in His heart and attitude—He actually HUMBLED HIMSELF. He voluntarily stepped down and gave up His good reputation to help others. It's a lot easier to give up possessions than to give up our good reputation. Sometimes God asks us to do that. We have our perfect example in Jesus. Only by His grace can we follow that amazing example.

2. I love the last few verses, which I copied in the second paragraph above. It begins with the word "Wherefore", which also means "therefore". Paul is clearly stating that the reason Jesus is so highly exalted now is because He first humbled Himself. We have no greater example than Jesus. He humbled Himself to help others and His Father rewarded Him with the highest honor He could ever bestow. If we humble ourselves in order to help others, God will also exalt us as He has promised.

3. I get really excited about this final point! As I shared in *The Boaz Blessing*, God is so amazing, in that He covers and forgives every single little thing that we ever do against Him or others if we just confess and ask for forgiveness. At the same time, He records and remembers every single little thing that we ever do for Him and others. Every time we humble ourselves in any little way to bless Him or others, it is written down and recorded for eternity. Wages and rewards are prepared for us according to how we have learned to humbly serve God and others.

SUGGESTIONS:

Here are some suggestions for guarding against the subtle intrusion of pride into your heart:

1. Keep a journal of answers to prayer and miracles that God has done for you. Read them often and give God glory.
2. Ask God to show you His heart for the poor around the world and in your neighborhood. You will focus more and more on serving others who are not as blessed as you.

3. Recognize the subtle ways the enemy tries to get us to compare ourselves with others to make ourselves feel superior. As I shared earlier, pride rose up in my heart as I looked at other students who had no passion to pray for the lost. Whether it's spiritual pride or social achievement, wealth, looks, fashion or any other aspect of life we could boast about, we need to resist all temptations to feel superior or judge others.

4. If you really want to develop humility and resist pride, ask someone to keep you accountable. Husbands and wives can work with each other in this. We often end up performing this function anyway for each other, so we may as well give each other permission to do it. Unmarried people can find a trusted friend and ask them to keep them accountable. Just say something like this: "I really want to kill my pride and would appreciate it if you would point out to me when you sense pride in what I do or say."

5. Don't give up when you feel like it's hopeless. Turn your feeling of weakness into an opportunity for God to reveal His strength. His strength is truly made perfect in our weakness. Humility is recognizing God's goodness in spite of our weaknesses.

Chapter Eight

The Greatest Shortcut to True Humility

You may fellowship in different religious circles, but if your eyes and ears are open in this day of easy access to information, you may have heard the testimonies of people who have had unusual special encounters with God. Some have had death or near-death experiences. Others have seen visions or dreams. Some have been in trances or actually felt transported to Heaven. Most people who have had these experiences have testified about how the presence of God stripped them of their pride and made them feel incredibly humble. Often they felt overwhelmed and unworthy to be in His presence.

Isaiah had such an experience in Isaiah 6. He was overwhelmed with the presence and glory of God and said,

> *"Woe is me, for I am undone! Because I am a man of unclean lips, and I dwell in the midst of a people of unclean*

lips; for my eyes have seen the King, the Lord of hosts."
(Isaiah 6:5)

Isaiah gained a great dose of humility when he encountered the Lord. Recently we read an article by Francis Frangipane as he shared an experience he had with God a number of years ago. In the brightness of God's glory he felt very unclean. He could see his selfishness and pride and missed opportunities to show the love of Jesus to others. At the same time, he felt nothing but love coming from the Lord. There was no judgment, only love. What he experienced was a great opportunity to understand and exercise humility.

We don't deserve God's love, but He gives it to us anyway through His grace. We just have to receive it and be thankful for it. That's what humility is all about. He gave me so much in spite of my failures and He even uses me and promotes me for letting Him extend His grace to others through the gifts He has given me. WOW! What an arrangement and what a great God we serve.

CAN *WE* ALSO HAVE AN ENCOUNTER WITH GOD LIKE ISAIAH AND OTHERS?

Are these supernatural encounters just for a few super-spiritual people and people in the Bible? To answer that, we should read the Beatitudes. The word "humility" is never used, but every verse relates in a special way to being humble.

I'd like to take a different approach to these beatitudes than the normal interpretation. I believe there is a progression of spiritual maturity and the fruit of humility as we move from the first beatitude till the last in Matthew 5:3-11. Let's read them first as they are written and then look at them from this different perspective.

Blessed are the pure in spirit, for theirs is the Kingdom of Heaven.

Blessed are those who mourn, for they shall be comforted.

Blessed are the meek, for they shall inherit the earth.

Blessed are those who hunger and thirst after righteousness, for they shall be filled.

Blessed are the poor in heart, for they shall see God.

Blessed are the peacemakers, for they shall be called the children of God.

Blessed are those who are persecuted for righteousness sake, for theirs is the kingdom of Heaven.

Blessed are you when they revile and persecute you and say all kinds of evil against you falsely for My sake."

The "poor in spirit" are the humble, who recognize how much of God they lack. Humility is where we begin the process of getting closer to God. The poor in spirit receive the Kingdom of Heaven. They can bring Heaven to earth.

"Those who mourn" are the humble, who feel their spiritual poverty and care about others who have been hurt by the enemy, and cry out to God for His touch and His comfort. They will be comforted by the presence of the Comforter, the Holy Spirit.

"The meek" are the humble who don't have selfish ambition for promotion. Because of their lack of selfish ambition God trusts them with dominion and authority on the earth.

Those who, "hunger and thirst after righteousness" are the humble folk who realize their own righteousness is like filthy rags. They want His righteousness, not their own. They will be filled with His righteousness.

The "merciful" are the humble who have been filled with His righteousness and now have His heart. They see people through God's eyes and extend His mercy to them. They will be given His mercy when they need it.

The "pure in heart" are the humble, who have gone through the above process and emptied their hearts as much as possible of its native iniquity and have filled their hearts with the purity of God's own heart. THESE ARE THE ONES WHO ARE PROMISED A SPECIAL GLIMPSE OF GOD IN THEIR LIVES. They don't all see God the same, but they do all see God.

The "peacemakers" are the humble who have seen God and know how much He loves unity in His family. They are on a mission to heal the hurts and bring peace where there is strife and conflict.

Those who are "persecuted" are the truly humble, who are willing to lay down their lives for the One Who laid down His life for them. Laying down our lives is one of the surest signs of true humility.

THE CYCLES OF HUMILITY

We stated at the beginning of this chapter that a shortcut to humility was to have an encounter with God. In the beatitudes we discovered that humility was the way to have an encounter with God. So which comes first—the chicken or the egg—humility or an encounter with God?

The fact is that God will usually give His special encounters to those who have already pursued humility. The encounter will then accelerate the process and deepen it, taking it to a new level of praise and worship for an amazing God. The heightened humility will lead to heightened encounters with God. It becomes a wonderful cycle and helps break the enemy's cycle.

That devilish cycle begins with insecurity, which leads to selfish, self-centered actions, followed by guilt and shame over our actions. This leads to more striving to impress others to compensate for a negative self-image, and more impure actions, followed by more guilt and shame.

We may not have the same kind of encounters as Isaiah, Peter and Paul, but we can definitely have our own uniquely designed encounters with God. He is waiting to reveal Himself. Remember, the pure in heart WILL see God.

The pure in heart are not those with perfect resumes. The pure in heart are those who long for Him to direct their thoughts and minds, those who want His will and His love more than anything in this world. The pure in heart will see God and the encounters will change them in wonderful ways.

As a friend and admirer of Heidi Baker, I don't know anyone who has articulated and demonstrated humility better than her. She teaches going "lower still," "going low and slow", "stopping for the one," "learning about the Kingdom from the poor and the children", "intimacy before performance," etc., etc. She doesn't just teach this kind of humility, she has demonstrated it for over forty years.

Another great apostolic teacher of intimacy with God is Mike Bickle. His teachings on the Song of Solomon have motivated tens of thousands to pursue intimacy and humility, and he has inspired thousands to open houses of prayer around the world to pursue this kind of intimacy through humility.

Chapter Nine

Humility and the Sermon on the Mount

The Sermon on the Mount begins with the beatitudes, but it doesn't end there. One can read the entire sermon in Matthew 5-7, and see how humility relates to virtually everything that Jesus talked about.

MATTHEW 5

After the Beatitudes, Jesus talks about true righteousness exceeding that of the Scribes and Pharisees, an obvious reference to their pride. Through God-given humility, which comes through His grace, we can actually have that kind of righteousness.

Jesus also talks about restoring relationships and marriage and divorce. Clearly, healthy relationships and good marriages depend on humility. Pride reacts to pride and produces strife and contention (Proverbs 13:10). On the other hand, humility attracts others to us and keeps relationships strong.

Jesus ends the chapter with an exhortation to love our enemies. That certainly requires humility. Our pride wants to get revenge, but humility wants healing and restoration of relationships.

MATTHEW 6

Jesus taught his disciples about fasting, prayer and giving. His focus is on doing these spiritual disciplines in secret, not showing off to others. It's another declaration of the importance of humility to God.

The "Lord's Prayer" reflects the thoughts and the heart of the humble man or woman. It gives great glory and honor to God and His Kingdom and expresses a strong dependence on God for provision for daily needs and forgiveness for sins, and for help to forgive others.

Much of the remainder of chapter six is devoted to not having earthly values, but seeking first the Kingdom of God. The proud don't find this easy to do. We need God's grace to humble ourselves to receive His heart so we can live for eternity, rather than this life.

MATTHEW 7

This chapter begins with the exhortation not to judge others. The humble do not judge, because they understand God's grace and see others through God's eyes. Jesus also exhorts His disciples to "Ask, Seek and Knock." The humble have no problem asking for help. They know how much they need it. The proud want to prove they can do it without help. That's why pride leads to destruction.

Much of chapter seven talks about the difference between those who appear to be righteous and those who really do God's will. The rewards are for the humble who know they need God's help and get the strength to do what God asks them to do.

FINAL THOUGHTS

I trust you have been convinced that humility is more than worth the effort it takes to pursue it. There is virtually nothing that God will withhold from us if He sees in us a pure and humble heart.

We were all born with pride. It's a universal disease we all have to deal with. We express it in different ways, but we all express it somehow or another. The Bible makes it clear that God hates pride. It was the first sin of Lucifer and the first sin of Adam and Eve. He knows that pride will lead us to destruction, so He allows situations to expose our pride so we can deal with it.

I certainly have not achieved humility to this day. I deal with my pride continuously. But after a few decades of this battle I can usually recognize when certain types of situations arise that God has just given me an opportunity to receive more grace. In those situations, I quickly see how powerful humility really is as a weapon of warfare with our enemy. But there are still other times when I have not realized what was happening and my pride has risen up in a fleshly response, thus causing me problems I didn't need. Both God and others resist me to some extent, when I react in pride.

You may thing this whole discussion on humility is an oversimplification of life, but I believe life is designed by God to be simple. Either we let our pride rule or we take the opposite course and go against our instincts to humble ourselves. The first response leads to pain and suffering, while the second response leads to healing and peace and love and other incredible blessings in His presence.

I don't know what your response will be to this information, but as for me, I want to experience the indescribable blessings of humility. Being taken into the presence of God and living with Him in Heavenly places, whatever that means exactly, sounds wonderful to me. Getting more grace and more anointing on the gifts He's given me sounds incredibly awesome as well. Having all my needs met, as He promises in Matthew 6:33, is another wonderful blessing. But being able to be a catalyst for revival and reformation in our society is one of the greatest blessings promised to those who first humble themselves and then follow through with God's instructions.

We need revival, reformation and restoration of all that we once had from God. The church once had incredible power and authority. Our nation once had high moral standards, which brought us great prosperity. Both America and the church will see the restoration of earlier glory if God's people humble themselves, pray, seek His face and turn from their wicked ways. Every nation can experience a move of God if His people will follow the same instructions.

Enjoy the journey! It may be rough at times, but the rewards are truly amazing!

About Ben Peters

BEN R. PETERS has been a student of the Word since he could read it for himself. He has a heritage of grandparents and parents who lived by faith and taught him the value of faith. That faith has produced many miracle answers to prayer in their family life. Ben and Brenda have founded a ministry in northern Illinois called Kingdom Sending Center.

They also travel extensively world-wide, teaching and ministering prophetically to thousands annually. Their books are available on most ereaders and all other normal book outlets, as well as their website:

www.kingdomsendingcenter.org

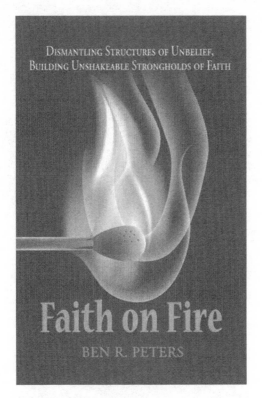

Faith on Fire
Dismantling Structures of Unbelief,
Building Unshakeable Strongholds of Faith
by Ben R. Peters

Available from Kingdom Sending Center
www.kingdomsendingcenter.org

"The Ultimate Convergence is imminent and I am excited with all that God is going to do." ~ Dr. C. Peter Wagner

BEN R. PETERS

The Ultimate Convergence
An End Times Prophecy of the Greatest
Shock and Awe Display Ever to Hit Planet Earth
by Ben R. Peters

Available from Kingdom Sending Center
www.kingdomsendingcenter.org

**Veggie Village and the Great
and Dangerous Jungle**
An Allegory
by Ben R. Peters

Available from Kingdom Sending Center
www.kingdomsendingcenter.org

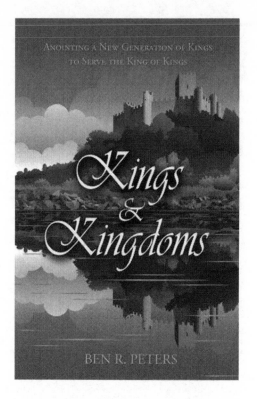

Kings and Kingdoms
Anointing a New Generation of Kings
to Serve the King of Kings
by Ben R. Peters

Available from Kingdom Sending Center
www.kingdomsendingcenter.org

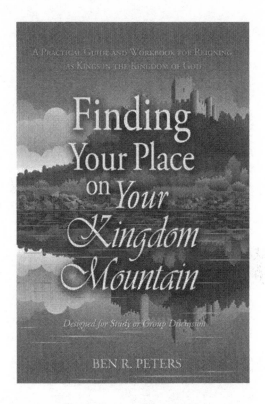

Finding Your Place
on Your Kingdom Mountain
A Practical Guide and Workbook for Reigning
as Kings in the Kingdom of God
by Ben R. Peters

Designed for Study or Group Discussion

Available from Kingdom Sending Center
www.kingdomsendingcenter.org

Catching up to the Third World
Seven Indispensable Keys
To EXPLOSIVE Revival
in the Western Church
by Ben R. Peters

Available from Kingdom Sending Center
www.kingdomsendingcenter.org

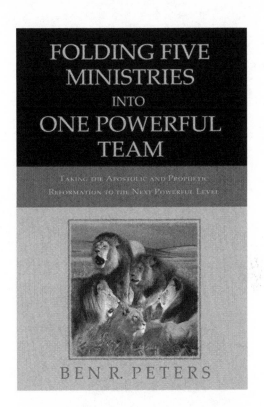

Folding Five Ministries Into
One Powerful Team
Taking the Apostolic and Prophetic Reformation
to the Next Powerful Level
by Ben R. Peters

Available from Kingdom Sending Center
www.kingdomsendingcenter.org

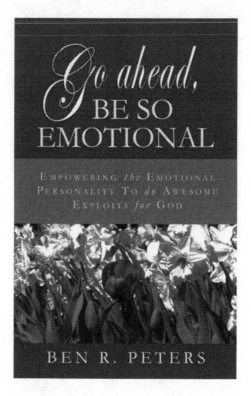

Go Ahead, Be So Emotional
Empowering the Emotional Personality
to do Awesome Exploits for God
by Ben R. Peters

Available from Kingdom Sending Center
www.kingdomsendingcenter.org

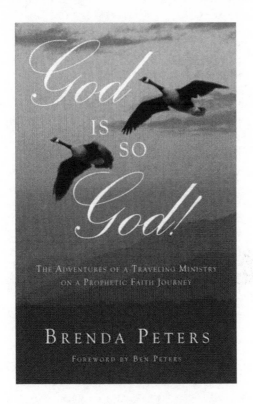

God Is So God!
The Adventures of a Traveling Ministry
on a Prophetic Faith Journey
by Brenda Peters

Available from Kingdom Sending Center
www.kingdomsendingcenter.org

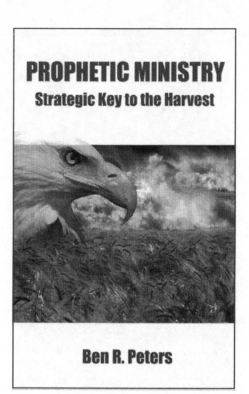

Prophetic Ministry
Strategic Key to the Harvest
by Ben R. Peters

Available from Kingdom Sending Center
www.kingdomsendingcenter.org

Resurrection!
A Manual for Raising the Dead
by Ben R. Peters

Available from Kingdom Sending Center
www.kingdomsendingcenter.org

Signs and Wonders
To Seek or Not to Seek
by Ben R. Peters

Available from Kingdom Sending Center
www.kingdomsendingcenter.org

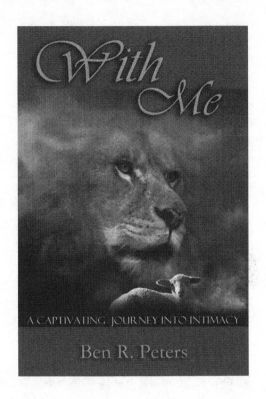

With Me
A Captivating Journey Into Intimacy
by Ben R. Peters

Available from Kingdom Sending Center
www.kingdomsendingcenter.org

Holy Passion: Desire on Fire
Igniting the Torch of Godly Passion
by Ben R. Peters

Available from Kingdom Sending Center
www.kingdomsendingcenter.org

Birthing the Book Within You
Inspiration and Practical Help
to Produce Your Own Book
by Ben R. Peters

Available from Kingdom Sending Center
www.kingdomsendingcenter.org

The Boaz Blessing
Releasing the Power of This Ancient Blessing
Into Your World Today
by Ben R. Peters

Available from Kingdom Sending Center
www.kingdomsendingcenter.org

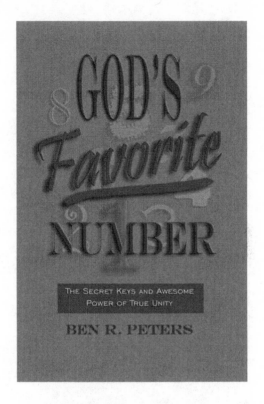

God's Favorite Number
The Secret Keys and Awesome
Power of True Unity
by Ben R. Peters

Available from Kingdom Sending Center
www.kingdomsendingcenter.org

92180590R00078

Made in the USA
San Bernardino, CA
30 October 2018